Medieval Holidays & Festivals

A Calendar of Celebrations

Madeleine Pelner Cosman

PIATKUS

To BARD

T.G.B.

whose love for living knows no seasons

First published in Great Britain in 1984 by
Judy Piatkus (Publishers) Limited
of London

Reprinted 1996

A catalogue record for this book is available from the British Library
ISBN 0 86188 400 0

Printed and bound in Great Britain by Bookcraft Ltd, Midsomer Norton

Welcome, Thanks, and Why
Some Chapters are Long and Others Short

Though holidays and festivals were important in medieval secular life, no dependable sources adequately describe them. Celebrations were too familiar to write about completely. Fifteenth century letters, for instance, recounting gorgeous Christmas costumes and gifts refer to games and feast treats only as "the customary ones." A special holiday play is called simply "the new one from France," and the music merely "the melodies we always sing." Information for this book, therefore, was acquired slowly—mostly in England, France, Italy, and Germany—and often from surprising sources. A holiday art question was answered in a scientific manuscript. A particular dance was best described in an angry cathedral sermon. The design on a castle's stained-glass window contained an original song lyric, and a delectable dessert recipe came from a 12th century text on asthma.

Such 12th through 16th century holiday lore accumulated until public spectacles and television cameras made this book inevitable. I direct a major academic program, the Institute for Medieval and Renaissance Studies, City College, City University of New York, as well as *Historic Spectaculars: the Complete Educational Entertainment Service,* which recreates medieval music, drama, art, science, and magic in theaters and classrooms, museums and shops, churches and temples, hospitals and homes. I also have a weekly television show called "Medieval Daily Life," which is a college course for credit and a cultural entertainment. Both the public and television audiences frequently request medieval presentations associated with familiar modern holidays. Winter and Spring calendar events are most in demand: December's Christmas, January's Twelfth Night, February's Valentine's Day, and June's Midsummer. In the Middle Ages these four also were among the most vivid, complex calendar festivals. Therefore, they have the longest chapters while the eight other months have short ones. However, holiday pleasures for all twelve months are added like "acts" to the basic theatrical event detailed in Chapter I, the "usual" fabulous medieval feast.

Enthusiastic young people from schools in New York City and its suburbs have shared such festivities: Students and teachers at Brearley, Dalton, New Lincoln, Chapin, Tottenville, New Rochelle, Port Chester, and School District 6; in New Jersey, Dwight Englewood School, Dwight Morrow, Elizabeth Morrow, Demarest, Closter, New Milford, Tenafly, Alpine, and particularly, the Humanities Program at Tenafly High School.

Young audiences have joined events I have run for gourmet societies such as the Confrérie de la Châine des Rôtisseurs, Les Dames d'Escoffier, the Wine and Food Society, and the Culinary Institute of America; for scholarly organizations such as The Cloisters, of the Metropolitan Museum of Art, and its Grace Rainey Rogers Auditorium, the History of Science Society, the New York Academy of Sciences, the New York Academy of Medicine, and the New York Botanical Gardens; and for businesses and philanthropies such as Bloomingdale's, Bamberger's, Abraham and Straus, banks, hospitals, libraries, and the Lighthouse for the Blind.

Several friends freely aided at need in New York, notably Lore Schirokauer, Dr. Arthur Tiedemann, Claudia Alston, Dr. Joan Kelley, Catherine Halligan, Ann McGavin, and Tina Penzel; Lillian Lenane, Cathy Armstrong, Dr. Hans Neuberg, Dr. DeWitt Goodman, Dr. William Ober, Dr. Carlton Chapman, and Dr. Al Lyons. I also benefitted from talks with Dr. William Darby in Nashville, Sharon King at WBZ in Boston, Dr. S. Kottek in Jerusalem, and in England, Sir Nikolaus Pevsner and Dr. Joseph Needham.

The first younger critic of this book was Michaela Elisabeth Donnelly of Toronto, whose sharp taste equals her mother's, Dr. Ruth Pelner Donnelly. The intelligent, nimble fingers that produced the typescript belong to Alexa Pierce.

Susan Urstadt cleverly introduced me to Charles Scribner's Sons' competent, congenial staff. Lee A. Deadrick, former Vice President and Editorial Director, welcomed this book and made its index. David Toberisky, Managing Editor; Marfé Ferguson, Editorial Assistant; Olga Richmond, Art Director; Marion Glick, Production Manager; and Clare Costello, Editorial Director, saw it through the press. All of us thank the six libraries graciously allowing manuscript and print illustrations: The New York Public's Spencer Collection, The Metropolitan Museum of Art, The Pierpont Morgan, The British Library, British Museum, and Galeria Medievalia.

My parents, Dr. and Mrs. Louis Pelner, my daughter Marin, and my son Bard Clifford have exulted in many medieval festivals. My husband, Dr. Bard Cosman, plastic surgeon and sculptor, best lives Yeats' ideal art of life: In custom and in ceremony are truth and beauty born.

Contents

v

CHAPTER I

The Glories of Medieval Celebration

Why Do People Celebrate? Why do people rejoice? Why should there be feasts and fasts and holidays? To the medieval mind, a good story was better than a direct answer:

Once upon a very long time ago, an old king before he died divided his kingdom exactly in half to give to his two sons. Each of the new young kings had the same amount of land, and people, and the same number of houses and farms. But the two kingdoms were different as night and day, for the young kings were opposite in every way. One was jealous, greedy, and cruel. The other was generous, gracious, and kind. As thoughtless and selfish was one, so thoughtful and selfless was the other. The evil king ruled the kingdom that was called Labora. The good monarch reigned over his kingdom, which was called Delecta.

One year the vicious king of Labora squinted at his subjects and said, "My people spend too much time in festivals and celebration. They enjoy holidays and do not work hard enough for me. I will banish all festivity from my kingdom. From now on there will be no birthdays, no music, no Christmas."

In the neighboring kingdom of Delecta, the generous king was so eager to please his people for their good work, he decreed that from that day forward every day would be a holiday. Work would be done by those who enjoyed it. No one would do more than a

---

Noblemen riding in procession are preceded by heralds playing fanfares.

fair share. Beautiful music, gorgeous feasts, elaborate costumes, favorite foods, and sweet cakes would be available to all on every day of the year.

In the first weeks after the decree, the people of Labora worked as hard as they could because of fear of their king. They had no pleasures at all. They grew sullen and thin. Nearby, in Delecta, the people rejoiced constantly, singing, dancing, and eating fine foods at all hours. They grew plump as they pleased themselves.

But after a year something terrible began to happen in both kingdoms. Labora's land and the people and animals were exhausted. They produced even fewer crops than before the "all-work-no-play" decree. In Delecta, too few people worked hard enough to make the land yield its grains, fruits, and vegetables. The animals, never properly fed, did not produce their young. The people of Delecta were so tired with the "all-play" policy that they no longer noticed the exquisite colors of the banners at parades. Nor did they hear the joyous sounds of the fanfares signaling new entertainments.

Suddenly both kingdoms were attacked by a fierce, fire-breathing dragon called the Terrible Tedium. This powerful dragon was so large and so foul that all the warriors with their bows and arrows were helpless against it. Every part of the dragon was protected by strong, steely scales. The Terrible Tedium burned and destroyed many people and much of the land in both kingdoms.

One late afternoon, the dragon started to shoot its stinking, fiery breath at each of the king's castles. The Terrible Tedium wanted to take the golden treasures of both kingdoms.

Labora's king hid himself in the innermost room of his castle. The good king of Delecta stood on a walkway near his castle's roof, surveying the devastation. The dragon came closer. Its scales rattled. It shrieked a high, piercing cry. It smelled like the foulest horrors of burning skin and metal. It lunged directly toward the king. Wearing his armor and pointing his bow, the king shouted, "What do you want in my kingdom?"

The dragon slowly circled, creaking its giant wings. The Terrible Tedium flew directly across the battlements facing the king. The leaves on the nearby trees immediately withered. All the soldiers shuddered and hid their heads beneath their shields. The good king, though trembling, stood his ground and shouted again, "Tell me what you want!"

The dragon wheeled around and shrieked. "Kiss me!" The astonished king summoned all his courage. He boldly walked close to the fuming dragon and put his lips to its loathsome neck. He kissed.

Suddenly, in place of the fierce, foul, ferocious creature there stood a beautiful young woman. She said, "Thank you. You have released me from an enchantment which made me destroy what I wished to preserve. My name is Festivity. I am the daughter of Queen Celebration. We are guardians of all holidays. We bring diversion and distraction to those struggling with life. We put markers on the road of time, allowing for things past to be remembered. In measuring time, we give hope for things future. We guard the birthdays, anniversaries, and holidays that make a person particular. We are life's balancers. We are life's rhythm-makers. Let me live once again as a welcome guest in your kingdom and in your brother's kingdom."

The young king of Delecta welcomed her joyfully and thereafter they lived long and merrily.

Festivity and celebration, then, do many good things for the mind and for the body. They provide recreation, reward, hope, and order. Without festivity, life can be tedious, repetitious, and dull. Even the most delectable treats stop being desirable if they can be had at any time. Work and play must beautifully balance.

The best way to understand a people is to study its celebrations. Few pieces of a past culture can reveal so much about it so quickly. More interesting than the adventures of important leaders or battles fought and won, feasts and festivals answer many significant questions. What did the people think beautiful? What was forbidden? What were the major sights of the daily life? The sounds? The tastes? The textures? The odors? What did the oldest people share with the youngest? What activities linked the most nobly born to the lowest? What was the people's ancient heritage? Did their culture cherish the past or reject it? What were the people's most important ideas? What was thought to be sacred? What did the people do for recreation?

Celebration is also important for recreating the past so that we can appreciate it better. By recreating a medieval festivity today we accomplish at least four things at once. We are reminded of the origins of certain modern ideas and customs, even such simple ones as how we hold a teacup or touch a daisy or measure a precious jewel. We learn more dramatically by recreation than by reading alone the answers to many questions that studying celebration reveals. We can also preserve beautiful ceremonies and actions, which otherwise would be lost. And we may find a few old customs lovely enough to impose permanently on our private lives. Selecting some ceremonies from our own past may help to dignify our own futures. For a short period, then, a medieval festival allows us not only to think medieval, but to live it.

Fabulous Feasts Suppose we are gathered for a fabulous medieval feast. We file into the banquet hall elegantly costumed in our velvets, silks, jewels, and brocades. Well-dressed young servants direct us toward our tables. The most noble guest or our host sits at the *high table*, raised above the others by a platform or *dais* so as to be able to see and to be seen by the guests. Behind the high table is a fancy canopy called a *baldaquin*, marking the place of honor. Everyone is seated according to social rank at long tables.

The *Surveyor of Ceremonies* is the feast hall's banquet master. The Surveyor carries a very large gold key attached to a heavy chain around his neck. He welcomes the guests with a hearty shout, "*Wassail, wassail, leavu freond*! Welcome, Welcome! Good cheer, dear friends!"

There are elaborate ceremonies before the exquisitely prepared foods are elegantly served. The medieval feast certainly is not coarse, crude food guzzled and gorged by graceless gluttons. Medieval feasting is theatrical ceremony. Just as important as the food's tastes and textures, so is their coloring and form. Dishes alternate with entertainment—food, then instrumental music; food, then song; food, then juggling; magic, mime, and minstrelsy; dancing and dramatic performance.

The Surveyor's Wassail The Surveyor of Ceremonies crosses the hall singing the wassail (welcome) song:

Here we go a-wassailing among the leaves so green,
Here we go a-wandering so fair to be seen.
Love and joy come to you
And to our wassail too;
And God send us a happy New Year!

Presentation of the Salt The Surveyor presents the *salt* to the guests at the *high table*. The salt is an elaborate, extravagantly shaped salt container. It has both practical and symbolic purpose. Salt, a most valuable spice, signifies rank. The most noble sits "above the salt." The other guests sit "below the salt." Remembering this ceremony, modern people often speak of a place of honor as "above the salt."

The Pantler Cuts the Upper Crust Next, the Surveyor waves his key to summon the *Pantler*. That noble servant is in charge of the bread. The Pantler wears a long, fringed fabric on his shoulder, called a *portpayne*, for ceremonially carrying loaves. The Pantler cuts the upper crust from a round, delicately spiced, beautifully colored loaf. Utilizing special knives, the Pantler horizontally cuts the top of the bread to present it to the most honored

From kitchen to banquet hall, cooks, a saucer, three servitors, and a carver present delicacies to the noble party.

guest. That demonstrates that he or she is the "upper crust," a phrase used even today for the most socially important people.

The breads are usually delicately colored: red with rose petal; green with parsley; gold with saffron. From such fragrant loaves the Pantler earlier would have fashioned the other guests' platters; individual metal or porcelain plates rarely are used. But edible, aromatic, practical "bread" platters called *trenchers* support the various finger foods. With sauces and gravies well absorbed, the trenchers make nutritious, delicious bread slices to eat at the meal's end, or they are toasted to eat at the next morning's breakfast, floating in wine. Sometimes the bread is offered to the eager resident dogs, or it is saved as a food gift, called *alms*, to be given to the poor waiting at the castle gate. A special servant called the *Almoner* collects such gifts in a huge bowl called the *alms dish*. He then distributes them to the needy.

The Laverer and the Aquamanile   The Surveyor now calls the *Laverer*. Bowing elegantly and twirling the fringes on a long, scarflike towel around his neck, the Laverer helps each guest to wash hands with spiced and herbed warm water. It is poured from a pitcher called an *aquamanile* into a bowl. The aquamanile

usually is amusingly shaped like a lion or dragon or wolf or griffin, whose mouth is the water spout. This hand-washing is not only for ceremony but for hygiene, because on the medieval table there are few spoons and knives and no forks. Rather, the most important table instruments are the strong, portable, manipulatable, practical extensions of the hands, the fingers. Every feaster eats with the fingers to assure that dining pleasure lingers.

Elegant finger etiquette determines which fingers are used for picking up meats, which for fish, which for fruit. Some fingers are kept extended for the dipping into spice dishes—the dried sweet basil, the cinnamon, the powdered mustard, and the brown sugar. Even today many people keep a pinky finger extended when holding a tea or coffee cup. Why? Because polite banquet rules imitate the medieval manner of keeping particular fingers free of sauces and gravies, the *spice fingers*. Table etiquette through the ages requires good finger choreography.

Credence Testing of the Drinks   After the Surveyor directs the wassail, the presentation of the salt, the cutting of the upper crust, as well as the making of the beautiful bread platters (the trenchers), and the ceremonial hand-washing using the aquamanile, several more table customs remain before a musical fanfare announces the first course.

The *Cup-Bearer* first must test the wine. The drink is poured by the master of the wine bottles and barrels, the *Butler*. This testing assures the host, noble guests, and feasters that the drink is pure and safe. The test is called *credence*, and is performed by tasting. Sometimes the test is chemical. A stone such as the *bezoar* is dropped into the fluid. It would change color if there were impurities or poison such as arsenic in the wine.

Wassailing and Blessing   Once the credence test is successfully completed, all the feasters raise their glasses to drink. The Surveyor exuberantly says once again, "Wassail, wassail! Drink well! To your health!" The banquet audience responds, "Wassail, wassail!" The resident clergyman blesses the food of the feast. Then the horns, trumpets, cornettes, shaums, drums, and bells play the fanfare signaling the service of the first of 17 or 29 or 77 or 127 courses.

Glorious Illusion Foods   At the fanfare's sound, the costumed servitors elegantly march each dish for presentation first before the *high table*. Then they proceed to serve each guest in descending order of social rank. The variety of tastes, textures, and food types is astonishing. All superbly prepared meats, fish, fowl, vegetables, fruits, and sweets are served for appearance as well as taste and fragrance. Beautifully feathered birds such as partridges, pheasants, and peacocks are roasted and then refeathered so that they look alive. Their claws and beaks gleam with painted gold. "Illusion" foods delight by surprising; they look as though they are one thing but truly are another. For example, "golden apples" are delicately spiced meatballs wrapped in gold-tinted pastry, with marzipan green leaves. "St. John's Urcheon" looks like a hedgehog but isn't—it is a whimsical animal sculpture made of meat and wrapped in brown carob pastry with edible quills. "Four and twenty blackbird pie," of course, is not filled with cooked birds. Perfectly safe for the tethered feathered ones within, the pie amazes guests when it is cut, liberating the birds to fly around the hall.

Subtleties   *Subtleties* also are dramatic festival foods. A subtletie is a large spun sugar, almond paste, marzipan, or pastry sculpture. It may be shaped like an animal, such as an elephant, lion, or fire-breathing dragon (when camphor and cotton in its mouth is set ablaze). Sometimes the edible statue may look like a great queen, or warrior, or pope, or a popular symbol like a peartree, gold star, or unicorn in a fenced garden.

Banquet Music   Feast music not only announces courses but serves as entertainment. Musicians either walk in procession preceding the servitors, or they play from a special musicians' gallery built high on a wall over the feasters' heads. Festival music, no matter how cheering or pleasing, also aids digestion. Therefore, music is played not only between but during certain courses. Some foods are thought better digested to particular melodies and rhythms. And birthday feasts and wedding banquets have specially stimulating mood music.

Astrological Temperament Food   Even the feasters' personalities determine the menu and order of food service. According to medieval astrology, a person's time of birth and zodiac sign affect physical appearance, intelligence, and attitudes toward living. The astrological sign, in turn, establishes the balance in the body among the *Four Humors*. These are the "vital fluids" that sustain life—blood, phlegm, yellow bile or choler, and black bile. These Four Humors determine the *Four Temperaments*. These are: the hopefully eager, or *sanguine*; the easy going, or *phlegmatic*; the excitable, or *choleric*; the sadly thoughtful, or *melancholic*. Food helps to keep these humors balanced. Therefore,

A young prince practices wine-pouring as he is taught the arts of cooking and serving, essentials of court etiquette.

feasts and festivals feature Astrological Temperament foods—meats and wines, herbs and spices, prepared to suit the individual reveler. The Surveyor introduces the *Chief Cook* to direct service of the Temperament dishes. These foods are thought important for health.

The Chief Cook   The Chief Cook walks and talks with authority. He wears a symbol of his office proudly around his neck: a long-handled tasting spoon swinging like a medallion from a heavy chain. He tests foods' quality and excellence by tasting. He also carries a large feather. This is a brush used for food painting.

If an elaborate, fanciful dish needs a last-minute decoration, his coloring brush is ready. The Chief Cook has two important duties: to protect health and to create food art.

The Carver In fact, every small part of the feast's preparation is done artfully. A *Carver* must cut meat into portions. But the Carver's motions are as graceful as a dancer's, with particular foot positions and bows required as accompaniment for various flourishings of the knives. Specially bladed and handled knives are held in proper finger positions for specific cuttings. Even the words are special for each animal carved: "Breaking a deer," "Unbracing a mallard," "Winging a partridge," and "Thying a pigeon."

The Warner Another banquet artist is the *Warner*. Like the chief cook, the Warner also carries a feather paint brush, and a curved knife. The Warner is the chief food sculptor who creates the subtleties. Sometimes these are paraded through the hall to "warn" guests that an important course is coming. Just as the subtleties often are called *Warners*, so are their creators.

Banquet Officers The medieval feast entertains all the senses. It is banquet theater. The Surveyor is both the chief actor and stage director who follows a carefully crafted script to please an important audience. All the other performers have precise parts, with well practiced entrances and exits. Each wears a costume suitable to social rank. Each carries an instrument that is both useful and a symbol of the profession. Here are twenty-two of the most common banquet officers who perform on the dining hall stage:

Officer	Symbol	Duty
Almoner	Large alms dish	Collecting and dispensing food gifts to the poor
*Butler	Large keys to wine cellar	Protecting and mixing wines

Officer	Symbol	Duty
Carver	Several knives	Carving meats at table
*Chief Cook	Tasting spoon and painting feather	Protecting feasters' health and creating food art
Cup Bearer	Tasting cup	Testing wines and drinks for purity and safety
Dresser	Tweezers or scissors	Arranging food on serving platters
Juggler	Balls, daggers, and rings	Feats of juggling
*Laverer	Aquamanile and fringed towel	Ceremonial hand-washing
Magician	Balls, scarves, and boxes	Feats of magic
Master of Venerie	Hunting horn	Presenting important game animals as hunt trophies
Mime	Mask	Performing wordless drama
Minstrel	Lute	Entertaining by songs
*Musician	Horn or stringed instrument	Performing fanfares, music for pleasure, melodies for digestion
*Page(s)	Small cap with feather	Directing guests to table and refilling drinking cups
*Pantler	Portpayne	Cutting upper crust and preparing trenchers
Patisser	Icing "comb"	Making and decorating pastry and cakes
Quistron	Heavy gloves	Turning spits for roasting meats
Rotisser	Long needles	Designing, preparing, and presenting roasted food
Saucer	Stirring spoon	Preparing sauces and glazes
*Servitor(s)	Baldric (a ribbon from shoulder to hip)	Ceremonially serving foods at table

*Surveyor of Ceremonies	Very large key	Directing all feast festivity
Warner	Painting feather and sculpturing knife	Creating subtleties

Naturally not every manor house has all these banquet performers, but many have most. Smaller halls have at least those banquet officers whose names are starred. However, certain jobs are easily combined. The Butler may also be the Cup Bearer, Pantler, and Carver. And when a troupe of mimes comes to town but magicians are in short supply, marvelous entertainment is made by the mimes; their magic is in silence.

A Typical Festival Feast   All these performers and careful ceremonies are for *usual* festivities. Each holiday adds special color and costume, particular seasonal foods and songs, games and rituals. Certainly Christmas in the medieval hall is unmistakably different from Midsummer Eve. But the particular holiday celebration is built upon the basic feast ceremony. Holiday celebrants simply add or subtract "acts" as required. For example, no Midsummer Eve is complete without a "St. George Play." For this holiday, then, a short, humorous drama substitutes for a more commonplace entertainment such as minstrelsy or magic.

Following is a typical, short, twelve-course feast. Portions are small and shaped to be eaten as easy, elegant finger food. The types of food are chosen for contrasts of color or design or spice. A sharp food alternates with a sweet, a lighter with a heavier, a delicately fragrant herb cake follows a heavily spiced meat. As always, a fanfare introduces each course. And the Surveyor of Ceremonies directs all rituals, such as wassail and credence.

The Surveyor's Ceremonies
1. Welcome Wassail and Presentation of the Salt
2. Cutting the Upper Crust
3. Credence Testing of the Wines
4. Hand-Washing with the Aquamanile

Course 1
Fruytes melior: plum, quince, apple, and pear with rosemary, basil, and rue in a pastry tart

Entertainment 1
Instrumental music by lutes, viols, krummhorns, bells, and drums

Course 2
St. John's Urcheon: a whimsical hedgehog sculpture of chopped meat wrapped in carob pastry (St. John's bread)

Entertainment 2
Merlin the Magician

Course 3
Almoundyn Eyroun: almond omelet with currants, honey, and saffron

Entertainment 3
The juggler with balls and daggers

Course 4
Saumon Rosted: roasted salmon in onion and wine sauce

Entertainment 4
Minstrels' songs

Course 5
Fruytes Royal Rice: artichokes filled with blueberry rice

Entertainment 5
Singers of ballads and street cries

Course 6
Aigredouncy: honey-glazed sliced chicken rolled with mustard, rosemary, and pine nut

Entertainment 6
Dancers performing joyous leaping dances, the *galliards*, and slow, stately *pavanes*

Course 7
Astrological Temperament Herb Cake

Entertainment 7
Mood music for the Four Humors

Course 8
Astrological Temperament Cheese

Entertainment 8
Songs for the Four Temperaments

Course 9
Dukess Wynges: roasted chicken and pheasant wings

Entertainment 9
Sword magic and levitation illusions

Course 10
Elderberry Divination Cakes: small crullers in imaginative shapes

Entertainment 10
Sir Gawain and the Green Knight Play

Course 11
Circletes y Roundels: small almond-spice cakes on *roundels*, platters with words or poems the guest must sing written on them

Entertainment 11
The Fire Juggler

Course 12
Parade of the Subtleties: ceremonial carving and eating of the sugar or pastry sculptures

Entertainment 12
Musical instruments honoring the season or the special guest. *Shawms* (horns with piercing, nasal sounds) signal the end of the feast.

The Invitation to Ingenuity   This, then, is the basic feast plan. For specific holidays, winter, spring, summer, or fall decorations are added. Particular structures are built, such as the *Maypole* or the *Midsummer candle circle*, or the *Christmas yule log*. Richest castle and poorest cottage share the same calendar of ceremonies. Of course, details differ. One Maypole is strung with gold and silken cords and crowned with a wreath of jewels. Another Maypole topped with daisies is wrapped with coarsest rope. But each is still a Maypole. The customs practiced round it are traditional, whether the reveler is a noble knight or a common carpenter.

Similarly, St. George's Midsummer Eve dragon must be amusingly terrifying. This dragon may be a magnificent machine that has mechanical wings and bellows smoke, an expensive marvel of engineering. Or a poor old blacksmith playing St. George may fight a homespun dragon-shaped kite held up by sticks and strings with a shepherd boy behind it. Young or old, royalty or craftsman, city mayor or country villager, all follow the same customary pattern for welcoming Midsummer.

Modern recreations of medieval festivals and holidays also ought to follow the basic patterns. Additions can be as rich or simple as time and cleverness allow. From the year's beginning until its end, from medieval New Year to Christmas, festivity and celebration gladden the spirit.

CHAPTER II

January: Twelfth Night

W HEN the evil King of Labora punished his people by decreeing all work and no pleasure, he banished one of their favorite holidays—Christmas. Therefore, he also forbade celebration of *Twelfth Night*, for medieval Christmas was not a single day but a twelve-day festivity. The Christmas finale was Twelfth Day, or more truly, Twelfth Night, the evening before. Celebrated on January 5, almost all of its remarkable customs revolved around contests.

Picture yourself amidst the revelry of Twelfth Night. The ceremonies cannot begin until a contest determines who will be *King and Queen of the Bean*. Luck rather than skill decides the winners. The answers are hidden in the *Twelfth Cake*. Most other foods and games, dances and entertainments also are ritual battles. A beautiful spiced cider, for example, is drunk while *Wassailing the Trees* to assure the triumph of the coming warm spring over the current cold winter. The *Oxhorn Dance* also is performed to bring good luck in the future seasons.

Twelfth Night revelers called *Mummers* perform short contest plays. A strong and good St. George must fight a powerful, evil knight. In the churches, Bible plays also depict battles between the good and bad. Three kings following a marvelous star must outsmart a wicked King Herod. These star-led noblemen are the Three Magi who bring gifts to the child whose birth signifies the true meaning of Christmas. Their visit gives Twelfth Night its other name: Epiphany Eve.

The King of Labora's banishing Twelfth Night certainly was a cruel punishment. Its costumes, disguises, stamping dances, hobby horses, tugs of war, festival flames, games, and feasts, as we shall see, made Twelfth Night one of the most magnificent winter holidays.

Disguises At most other feasts, the guests are dressed in their usual medieval finery. On Twelfth Night they add eye masks to their costumes. Some revelers will have important roles to play in the Twelfth Night pageantry. They wear disguises. At least six people wear hats topped with large antlers or horns, and small bells around the ankles of their boots. One guest is dressed as the warrior knight, St. George. Another looks like a hobby horse, complete with mane and tail. One Twelfth Night merry-maker is costumed in orange from hat down to shoes. A large letter "O" for Orange is sewn to the front of the tunic. Another is clothed entirely in bright yellow, wearing an ornamental "L" for Lemon. They are the team leaders for the contest game Oranges and Lemons.

The only person not masked is the Surveyor of Ceremonies. Everyone is in the "guise" of someone else. For displaying the clever masks and disguises, a *guise procession* is the first festivity.

The Guise Procession The Surveyor signals the musicians to sound a fanfare. Each guest joins in line behind the Surveyor. To a slow, stately melody, everyone walks in rhythm in a large circle around the hall. Guests quietly perform gestures appropriate to their disguises. The Fighter flourishes a mock sword. The Horse trots. The horned animals stamp. The Three Kings from the Orient proudly carry elaborate gift boxes. After three circlings of the room, the Surveyor leads the guests to their seats. The feast ceremonies now begin.

The Surveyor welcomes bird-masked mummers to a ladies' feast while musicians play.

The King and Queen of the Bean   Every medieval festival starts with the Surveyor performing the welcome wassail. The ceremonies are directed particularly to the most important guests seated at the high table. But on Twelfth Night the high table is empty, at least temporarily. The Surveyor sings the wassail song to all in the hall. But it is not possible to present the salt or upper crust or to perform the rituals of credence or hand-washing. On Twelfth Night, the places of honor at the high table are taken not by the noblest nor the richest. The most honored revelers are the King and Queen of the Bean. They must be chosen, with the help of the Twelfth Cake.

Twelfth Cake   On the high table is a very large, somewhat flat, circular cake, the Twelfth Cake. In French it is called the Kings' Cake: *gâteau des rois* or *galette des rois*. Usually there are two identical Twelfth Cakes. Baked within the first is a single, large, dried bean. In the most elegant kitchens the baker inserts a precious gold, porcelain, or unbreakable glass "bean." The cake is carefully cut and each of the men feasters is served a small piece. The finder of the Bean in his portion is King of the Bean and Master of the Twelfth Night revels.

Baked into the second cake, served only to the women, is a large dried pea. Imitating that vegetable, wealthy bakers use a small jewel or valuable pea-shaped party favor. The woman finding this pea in her piece of Twelfth Cake is called Queen of the Pea or Queen of the Bean.

Once the King and Queen of the Bean are selected, the musicians play a lively march while the Surveyor seats the new master and mistress of Twelfth Night at the high table. The King and Queen remove their masks. Each receives a small crown and a sceptor. Now the Surveyor honors them with the salt, the upper crust, the credence cup, and the hand-washing with the aquamanile. The Surveyor then shouts the usual hearty "Wassail!" On Twelfth Night, however, not only the people are wassailed—so are trees.

Wassailing the Trees   After the first beautiful foods are served, the guests must wassail the trees. Farmers and country folk bundle up in coats and cloaks, leaving the warmth of the hall for the orchard or forest. There among the fruit trees they perform a wassail ceremony around the largest, oldest tree, or the one bearing the most fruit during the year.

However, other Twelfth Night celebrants wassail a tree in the hall. A large apple-tree sculpture is made of papier-mâché or metal, or it is an edible marzipan subtletie fruit tree. Sometimes, a young live tree is uprooted and brought indoors, just as a modern Christmas tree might be. The tree is securely set in a large tub in the center of the room so there is enough space left for dancing around it.

Twelve wassailers surround the tree, forming a circle. They carry large glasses, or *tankards*. These are half-filled with apple cider, with three small pieces of toasted caraway seed cake floating on the surface. Rhythmically, the wassailers walk around the tree, chanting this rhyme:

> Hail to thee, old apple tree!
> From every bough
> Give us apples enow;
> Hatsful, capsful,
> Bushel, bushel, sacksful,
> And our arms full, too.

Lifting their glasses to the tree, they toast it and shout wassail. They take a few sips of the cider. Then each eats one piece of the seed cake and places the other two on the branches of the tree or below it in the tub. A second time they slowly march around the tree, repeating the rhyme. At this circling, the tree drinks. Each wassailer pours the remaining cider into the tub surrounding the tree's roots. A third chanting procession around the tree ends with wild shouts of "hurrah," stamping, shaking of noise makers, and banging of the empty cider tankards.

The purpose of this amusing, noisy ritual is to ensure plenty of good cider to fill the cups next year. Wassailing fruit trees is a folk charm for a bountiful harvest. It encourages the trees to bear many a plum and many a pear. The cakes and cider are food gifts for the trees' guardian spirits. The noise and stamping are for startling slumbering tree spirits who might be forgetful of the need to awaken at the coming of spring.

Lamb's Wool People and trees drink varieties of Twelfth Night apple cider; one such splendid drink is *Lamb's Wool*. It is cider (or wine or beer) heated with sugar, nutmeg, and ginger, with roasted apples floating on the surface. The soft apple pulp bursting from the skin looks white and frothy or woolly like a lamb. Lamb's Wool with crabs is a favorite variety. Spiny clawed animals are not the ingredients, though; instead, rather tart crab apples are used. Lamb's Wool can be drunk at any time during the feast. But it is especially important at the *Twelfth Night fires*.

Twelfth Night Fires   At outdoor country celebrations, at least one drink or food is served around the Twelfth Night fires. In an open field sown with twelve rows of wheat, twelve very small straw fires are built, plus one large fire. Around this the revelers gather. Indoors, candles are substitutes for fires. In a darkened hall, twelve candles or sets of candles in sturdy holders are lit, one by one. The guests shout wassail at the lighting of each. Three candles are evenly spaced in each of the four corners of the room. A very large candle or candelabrum with several candlesticks makes the largest fire. This thirteenth fire is sometimes called *Old Meg*. In field or hall, this Twelfth Night fire is the centerpiece for cheerful drinks and songs.

What do these Twelfth Night fires signify? Some say they are supposed to assure the health of the next harvest, and that they are burnt grain offerings to the spirits of the fields. Others find purely Christian origins for the twelve fires. One each is for the twelve days of Christmas, the largest and last fire dedicated to Christ himself. Some think of the fires as representing the twelve Apostles plus Jesus; or the twelve Apostles surrounding the Virgin Mary.

Perhaps all of these explanations are correct. Old pagan myths and fertility rituals often are adopted by Christians and put to new purposes. Spring and summer holidays such as Midsummer Eve have festival fires called bonfires. Originally these were built to honor a pagan sun god. Later the lights were used to praise St. John the Baptist.

To the medieval mind, that past pagan heritage is believed

important. The rituals for fertility of crops and trees and animals are not necessarily rooted in superstition or evil, but they are incomplete. Medieval religion gives "true" meaning and purpose to those old ideas. Some older religious customs, as such, are cherished. People enjoy them. People find them comfortably familiar. But the customs are rededicated; the Christian saint is substituted for the pagan god. A favorite pagan animal ritual becomes a Christian Twelfth Night treat called the Oxhorn Dance.

Oxhorn Cake and Oxhorn Dance   After several feast courses are served, six people disguised as "oxen," wearing horned head-dresses and belled boots, circle around the wassail tree. While the musicians play a march, they stamp vigorously in procession. The small bells on their boots ring the rhythm. The Surveyor asks the King and Queen of the Bean to select the finest ox, the *Best Beast*. On one of this ox's horns, the Surveyor places a firm round cake with a hole in the middle. This oxhorn cake is made of oats, caraway seeds, and currants. (A papier-mâché cake serves equally well.) The ox must dance to throw off the cake. It requires amusing, often ridiculous head movements. The other five "ox" revelers imitate the Best Beast. Every one in the hall makes a silent bet as to which direction the oxhorn cake will fall. If it falls in front of the animal, it is called the *Boosey*. If it falls behind, it is called the *Istress*.

Every guest then is served a miniature oxhorn cake, resembling a seed and raisin doughnut. Each servitor carries one tray each of Boosey and Istress. The feaster eats the cake betted upon.

All of this revelry may seem like strange nonsense. The animal stamping dance is a thousands-of-years-old reminder to the earth's spirits to triumph over winter by reawakening in spring time. Since people's survival depends upon animals themselves being powerful and plentiful, the oxhorn cake is a stimulating gift for the animals' spirits. These fertility customs are far older than Christianity. But medieval churches encourage the ancient popular oxhorn dances. Some even store the horned headdresses between one Twelfth Night and the next. Why? Because the oxen and beasts of the field were friends to the infant Jesus born in their stable. As they shared warmth and home on the first Christmas, so these beasts deserve celebration on all later Twelfth Nights of Christmas.

The Hobby Horse   Suddenly a loud neighing of a horse is heard in the hall. In response, musicians imitate horse "neighs" and "snorts." Then the Horse itself trots in. It canters up to the King and Queen of the Bean at the high table. It bows in fancy patterns. It gallops, walks, proudly slings its tail to right and left. Then, it speaks! For this horse is a beloved feature of many folk rituals. It is a character of pageantry in both the village and the court. In simpler country ceremonies, a rustic man may ride a broomstick with a painted wooden horsehead and a rough rope and bell for bridle. In a courtly festivity, a Hobby Horse has expensively embroidered blankets on a wicker and wire body and flank, which surrounds the "rider." Human legs propel the animal. Jewel-encrusted reins direct the horse's head, whose eyes are precious stones and whose mane is woven gold. The appearance of either kind of Hobby Horse always signals "a marvel to come."

Mummers' Mummings   The Twelfth Night Hobby Horse usually is a *Mummer*. Mummers are country or town folk who act in traditional holiday theatricals called *mummings* or *mumming plays*. Rarely are they professional performers. Rarely are they nobly born. Rarely are they well educated. But sometimes they are all three. Almost always they are affectionately welcomed no matter how simple the audience or how sophisticated. For each year the Mummers perform plays so old their beginnings are not remembered. Some of the plays' meanings are not understood. Sometimes their drama is so simple, it seems silly. But year after year and age to age, they delight. Mummings are both familiar and strange at the same time. The Hobby Horse always prances at Twelfth Night. Good St. George is always killed and then revived from the dead by a peculiar old doctor. Mummings seen each year give that special thrill of the well-known unknown.

A Mummers' Play of St. George

[*First the Hobby Horse speaks.*]

HOBBY HORSE: With gallant St. George I always ride.
Weather now is so cold, we must come inside.
Give us this room to act our play.
England's own King will clear the way.

Then follows an amusing contest play. The characters are:

1. The King of England
2. Prince George, his son
3. A Turkish Knight
4. The Noble Doctor
5. A Clown

The King enters first. Then each character introduces himself with the traditional beginning: "I am . . ." Naturally the audience already knows who is who. It knows who will fall, who will fail, who will triumph, who will prevail. The guests know well that St. George once killed a fierce dragon and rescued a princess, for that adventure is the subject of a Midsummer mumming play. The familiar humor of a Twelfth Night St. George play resembles this:

THE KING: I am the King of England.
To you I boldly now appear.
I come to seek my only son.
Yet I fear for the Prince.
My son is here!

PRINCE GEORGE: I am Prince George, a most worthy knight.
I will spend my blood for England's right.
England's right I always maintain,
I'll fight! I would die for England's fame!

TURKISH KNIGHT: I am the Turkish champion.
    From far off Eastern lands I come.
    I'll fight old England's King, and then
    Kill off the best of all his men.

PRINCE GEORGE: I am Prince George, the champion bold.
    My sword and I won three crowns of gold.
    I slew the fiery dragon, and kept from slaughter
    The King of Egypt's only daughter.

[With a swagger and a sneer, the Turkish Knight points to St. George's sword.] He says:

TURKISH KNIGHT: I heard a lady cry, "A fool!"
    A fool! That was her every word.
    "Surely that man is a fool
    Who only wears a wooden sword!"

[Prince George, hearing this insult, accepts the challenge to fight. Drawing his strong sword, he lunges toward the Turkish Knight, who has his weapon ready.]

PRINCE GEORGE: Stand off! Stand off! Here is a surprise.
    By my strong hand and sword you'll die.
    I will cut you down to size.
    Prepare for your blood and your life to fly!

[Prince George nearly kills the Turkish Knight. At the last moment, the Turkish Knight tricks the Prince and seriously wounds him. The old King shouts, "Ruined! Ruined!" Then he runs to look for a doctor to save his son from his deep and deadly wound. Suddenly, in walks the noble doctor.]

NOBLE DOCTOR: I can cure all sorts of diseases
    Whatever hurts, whatever displeases.
    I can cure the itch, the stitch,
    Paralysis, palsy, and the gout.
    And if the devil is in a man
    My wit and I can fetch him out.
    By the word of my command
    I will make this Prince now stand.

Saint George raises his sword for a final death blow to the dragon.

[*He shouts, "Arise! Arise!" Prince George obeys and leaps up healed and well. He bows to the Doctor, and then, flourishing his sword, also bows to the audience. At that moment, the Clown rushes in with sommersaults and buffoonery. He offers his pointed cap, upside down, to collect coins from the audience. He says, "In comes I who has never been yet!" The Clown, Prince, King, Turk, Doctor, and Hobby Horse chant:*]

Our revels now are done.
They and we must be gone.
Till Christmas Twelfth another year
Good luck, good cheer! And we will be here!

Oranges and Lemons   But the Twelfth Night merrymaking is not yet over. Though the Mummers leave the center of the hall, feasting and entertainments continue. At midnight a more serious battle play will welcome the Twelfth Day of Christmas. Before that, however, there are more ritual battle games. One is Oranges and Lemons.

The Surveyor summons the Twelfth Night guest who is dressed in Orange. Then he calls for Lemon. The two "colors" face one another and raise their arms to join hands in a pointed arch. Everyone in the hall is invited to play.

"Prisoners" are captured for each team, the Orange or the Lemon. Each guest marches in a long line beneath the arch. All sing a song about English church bells. However, the song of Oranges and Lemons has a surprising last line: "Here comes a chopper to chop off your head!" At that last word, the "arch" falls and catches a "prisoner," who must choose to stand behind either the leader of Orange or Lemon. The song repeats until everyone is on one team or the other. Then there is a friendly tug of war. The winning team is called Spring. The losers are Winter. Each "prisoner" is the "sacrifice" that allows the triumph of the new season.

This is the song:

Oranges and Lemons!
Say the Bells of St. Clements;
You owe me five farthings,
Say the Bells of St. Martin's.
When will you pay me?
Say the Bells of Old Bailey.
When I grow rich,
Say the Bells of Shoreditch.
When will that be?
Say the Bells of Stepney.
I'm sure I don't know,
Says the great Bell of Bow.
Here comes a candle to light you to bed.
Here comes a chopper to chop off your head!
Last, last, last, last, last man's head!

The star over the manger in Bethlehem directs the Three Kings traveling with gifts.

The Three Kings' Star Happily exhausted, Twelfth Night celebrants know a final ceremony will send them home thinking of Christmas. All the candles and lights in the hall are snuffed out. A brilliant "star" mysteriously moves across the "sky." This is the Star of Bethlehem leading the Three Kings to Christ's cradle.

The star is a circular candelabrum or chandelier moved by mechanical pulleys and ropes invisible in the darkened room. Sometimes the star is polished, faceted glass, crystal, or silver, which reflects candlelight from below. Sometimes a simple circle of candles is held aloft on a tall pole. Its mover cannot be seen in the dark hall.

Guests or actors then enact the Biblical story of the Three Kings and their three gifts. Star-led, the Three Kings carry candles and presents. Marveling, they follow the star. They are stopped by an arrogant, blustering King Herod who fears his power will be destroyed by the infant destined to become the greatest of kings.

Herod tries to trick the three Magi into revealing the place where the baby is hidden.

Cleverly outwitting King Herod, the three wealthy monarchs from the Orient reach the poor stable. There they present, first, a gift of gold, honoring kingship. Second is the gift of the spice frankincense, suitable for a God. Third is the gift of the herb called myrrh, which stands for mortality. This playlet at midnight introduces the new day, called Twelfth Day of Christmas or Epiphany. It celebrates the joyous revelation that a King of Kings is born.

Twelfth Night, like the Twelfth Day following, is the holiday of hope. After darkness comes light. After the dead of winter comes sunny, exuberant spring. After sorrow there is joy.

While musicians play, a servitor presents three covered dishes to the king, queen, and guests.

CHAPTER III

February: St. Valentine's Day

FEASTING in February on rare roast beef in golden pastry, and roasted chestnuts and cream, St. Valentine's celebrants expect to be in the mood for love. These holiday meats and fruits are special *foods of love*. Decorations in the hall are *love lanterns*. Costumes have love ornaments called *love-knot* jewelry and *love sleeves*. Music stimulates amorous ideas. Entertainments pair people with one another for ritual courtship. Games such as *Lady Anne* and *King William* require selecting a partner who represents the mate for marrying. Love poems, love letters, and love plays also honor St. Valentine.

Amazingly, no one knows for sure who St. Valentine was or how his name and love were joined. At least three saints are named Valentine. Stories tell of their deeds or of their deaths on February 14 in the second and third centuries. Somehow their names have been linked to love, along with the names of Cupid and Venus. Venus, the mythical goddess of Love, is the mother of the winged blind boy, Cupid, who mischievously shoots the arrows that cause people to fall in love "at first sight." People pierced through their hearts by Cupid's arrows become one another's *Valentines*. They send each other love notes which are called *Valentines*. The wonderful ceremonies in February are known as *Valentinings*.

St. Valentine's Day is said to be the world's favorite wedding day. It is thought in nature to be the time that the birds choose their mates. In imitation, then, people must celebrate this natural season for love.

Love Lanterns and Fragrant Decorations in the Hall   Even before seeing the Valentine's decorations in the hall, one smells them. Gorgeous fragrances come from the rosemary, basil, marjoram, yarrow, and bay leaves. These crushed herbs float on rosewater in small bowls, at least one on each table. Some candles have spices in the wax and release the odors as they burn. Not far from the high table, an incense burner swings with the fresh sweet smell of laurel and pine.

Love lanterns give a soft, gentle light. These are vegetable candle holders. Resembling Halloween jack-o-lanterns, the Valentine lights are large, hollowed-out turnips or similarly firm vegetables or fruits. A smiling face is cut through the skin, piercing to the now empty center. A thick candle is set inside and lighted. Stiff paper, ceramic, or silver love lanterns work equally well.

Love-Knot Jewelry and the Crowned "A"   A guest wears at least one love token. A usual piece of jewelry is a small metal pin worn at the collar or over the heart, called a love-knot. Shaped like the number 8 resting on its side, ∞, the love knot represents the perfection of an affection without beginning and without end. When made of gold, the metal which never tarnishes and therefore never "dies," it signifies eternal love. Love knots sometimes are cut from gold fabric and sewn on the Valentine costume.

Another woven gold emblem of love is the crowned "A." Usually worn on the chest, or as a metal clasp for a cloak, a capital "A" is topped by a royal crown. This stands for the famous Latin tribute to Love's power: *amor vincit omnia.* It means "love (*amor*) conquers (*vincit*) all (*omnia*)." Either the emotion called love, or the blind God of Love, Cupid, is the crowned king of all human life. No one is strong enough to withstand the might of love.

Love Sleeves   Still another costume decoration is a love sleeve. Medieval garments usually have detachable sleeves. This is as practical as it is fashionable. It allows laundering of the parts of the costume most likely to get soiled by spills or by sweat. The velvets, embroideries, brocades, and fur-trimmed garments then can be cleaned as needed, but less frequently than the sleeves. Many a knight goes into battle carrying his beloved's sleeve on his shield for good luck. On Valentine's Day, many a lover wears the distinctive sleeve belonging to his or her favorite friend. For medieval sleeves are a part of the costume made to the order of the wearer no matter what the general fashion. Although a particular gown or tunic design is "in style," the color of the sleeve and the shape usually depend upon the wearer's whimsy.

A woman may be fond of wearing green sleeves with her clothes. Honoring this habit, she may be called by the secret affectionate name of Greensleeves. One of the most famous English ballads, in fact, is addressed to just such a woman: my lady Greensleeves.

This gives yet another meaning to the expression, "he wears his heart on his sleeve." The man wearing his beloved's sleeve over his own or in place of his own truly displays the affection of his heart for all the world to see.

Wearing the Heart   But there is a literal meaning for the expression "wearing the heart." A red heart cut from fabric or enameled onto metal is sewn or pinned onto the front of a garment or onto the sleeve. It is a sign that the wearer is devoted to Love. This love may be for a particularly wonderful person, or the idea of love, or the God of Love, or the Saint of Love, St. Valentine.

Love Music: The Chivaree   The guests file into the banquet hall to the sound of stimulating music. The melodies and rhythms are designed to lift the spirits and create the mood for love. Some Valentine melodies imitate the songs of birds. A particular type

The two lovers embracing wear love tokens: his, at right, is a love sleeve; hers, a love-jewel necklace.

of Valentine music resembling the music for a wedding feast is called the *chivaree*. Musicians play stirring horn melodies with a strong beat, like a march tempo, with increases in intensity of sounds, called *crescendos*. This love music is meant to arouse listeners to a thrill of pleasure.

The Surveyor's Wassail and the Valentine Cup As the guests are seated to the sound of the *chivaree,* the Surveyor performs the usual welcome wassail at the high table. However, an extra ceremony is added to the rituals of the salt, bread, hand-washing, and credence. The Surveyor has the Butler or the Cup-Bearer fill a large tankard and place it in a most visible position on the high table. Then the Butler will elegantly bow, not only to the honored guests, but to the cup itself. This is the Valentine Cup. It is meant for the Spirit of Love, which everyone wants to welcome into the hall. The guests rise, holding high their own glasses. The surveyor shouts, "To Love! *Amor vincit omnia!*" The audience repeats this tribute. All then are seated.

Lovers by Lot   At all other feasts, guests expect to see a bread platter at each place. On Valentine's Day there is a golden-colored bread trencher—tinted and spiced with saffron—between every *two* places. These trenchers are to be shared, each by a pair of Valentines. So before the guests can eat, they must be paired off.

This is a light-hearted game among friends. It does not matter whether one has a true lover or not. This is a public celebration

Scribes prepare a list, as if for lovers by lot, while banquet service begins at the high table.

of a season for love. So every guest, young or old, married or maiden, is given a Valentine lover by lot.

At each table, someone is appointed the scribe. He or she writes with a feather quill pen the name of one guest each on a small paper square. Each of these is a "lot." Folded in half, the lots are placed in a drawstring bag or glass bowl which is passed clockwise around the table. A guest selects a lot, throwing back the name of someone of the same sex, until everyone is paired.

Once lovers are chosen by lot, they exchange places with other guests until every pair is seated, ready to share a Valentine trencher. Lovers by lot may be *nonce lovers*; that is, together only for the duration of the feast. But sometimes lovers exchange gifts and attentions for a whole year. The Valentine service of love ends the following February 14 at the next love feast. Whatever type of lovers-by-lot are chosen, the Surveyor now signals the musicians to sound a fanfare for the first foods of love.

Foods of Love Various meats, fish, birds, eggs, vegetables, fruits, spices, and wines are thought to stimulate affection. Peacock is elegantly served. It is roasted and then refeathered; with camphor and cotton in its mouth set ablaze, it appears to breathe fire. Roasted partridge and stewed quail also quicken the Valentine emotions. At least one feast dish must be made of eggs, and not only chicken eggs. Other birds' eggs are sensual to eat, particularly those from geese, pheasant, quail, and sparrow. However, eggs are also thought to cause freckles! So they are eaten in omelets with chopped almonds, which prevent freckling.

Fruits that have seeds are important foods of love. Apples have been associated with love since the Biblical Garden of Eden. Sweet pears are the favorite of the goddess Venus. And every Valentine table serves those abundantly seedy fruits, figs and pomegranates.

Plum Shuttles, Heart Cakes, and Cooling Salads Delicate red and purple cakes are important feast fare. *Plum shuttles* are long, finger-length oval cakes made with purple plums, currants, and caraway seeds. They resemble the shuttles that weavers use to guide the threads through the warp and weft of cloth. The cakes signify the "weaving" of love into the "fabric" of life.

Small, heart-shaped cakes are made with a red fruit, such as cherries, plums, or pomegranates. Feasters eat these to celebrate "heartfelt" feeling.

With good humor, everyone eats to delight in the mood of love. St. Valentine's love, however, is more whimsical than serious in spirit. Just as there are foods for passion, so there are foods to counter-balance it. Certain vegetables cool and quiet emotions. The best cooling salad is made from lettuce tossed with the herbs fennel, chicory, and rue.

A Valentine Guessing Game: Lady Anne   The paired lovers for the feast are forgotten during Valentine guessing games. One is called Lady Anne. It requires guests to sit on chairs facing one another in a tight circle. One who is the Lover stands within the circle. Each guest must pass a small ball one to another with hands behind their backs. The Lover must not see who has the ball but must guess. The true holder of the ball is the Lover's beloved Valentine. The game disguises a Valentine who is only revealed by the Lover's correct identification of a "sign of love."

The Lover in the ring holds a glove, and chants:

Here we come a-piping
First in February, then in May.
My lady (or my good sir) sits upon the throne
Bright as a jewel I call my own.
Here is a glove to cover the hand
Of the best Valentine in all the land.
I choose but one, I choose from all,
I pray dear lady (or dear sir) yield me the ball!

If the Lover guesses wrongly and offers the glove to one who does *not* have the ball, this wrong person says:

The ball is mine and none of thine.
And so, good morrow, Valentine!

The Lover must exchange places with this "wrong" person who now becomes the Lover and holds the glove. The ball continues to be passed behind the backs to the accompaniment of the chant: "Here we come a-piping."

But if the Lover guesses correctly, the Beloved replies:

This ball is yours and none of mine.
I choose you as my Valentine!

And that Lover and Beloved couple now leave the circle. The game continues until everybody is a member of a pair of Valentines.

Another Pairing Game: Lord William A simpler pairing game is Lord William. Everyone sits in a large circle facing toward the center. One Lover stands within and walks around slowly, observing the players. They all chant the verse: "Lord William." At the last word—"heart"—the lover selects a Valentine. The chant goes like this:

Lord William was Lord David's son.
All the royal race is run.
Choose from the East,
Choose from the West,
Choose the one you love the best.
If she (or he) is not here to take her (or his) part,
Choose another with all your heart!

These two Valentines briefly kiss on the cheek and, arm in arm, walk within the circle.

The other players repeat the Lord William chant. At the word "heart" each of the Valentine's pair chooses another "mate." Now two couples walk within the slowly diminishing circle of guests. And the rest chant again. There is a new exchange of lovers at the sound of the word "heart." The game ends when everyone has been chosen at least once as a partner.

Musical instruments accompanying festivals
include organ, harp, table harpsichord, viol,
krummhorn, recorders, lute, and drums.

Love Divinations   Valentine's Day is the time for questions
about love. Certainly one of the most powerful human emotions,
it is one of the most uncertain. Anyone thinking seriously about
passion asks at some time such questions as these: How do I
recognize a true love? Who would make the best beloved? Who
is my true love? Where will I find someone to love? When? Will
this love last long? How do I make love endure? One medieval
method of obtaining answers is by *divination*.

Divination is the attempt to discover answers to important questions about the past or present or future. Commonplace objects,
when studied "correctly," will reveal answers by hint and clue. But
one must learn how to read them. On Midsummer Eve, for example, it is customary to inquire whether one's lover truly loves or
not. The divination object is a flower. A Midsummer rose is picked
and examined petal by petal. Each petal, however, reveals an
opposite answer. Either he loves me; or he loves me not. Only the
last petal reveals the beautiful or terrible truth.

Divining by Hemp Seed   A St. Valentine's divination reveals the identity of a future wife or husband. Common *hemp seed* is used for the divination. Four questioners, eager for their answers, stand in the middle of the hall. Each carries a small bag of hemp seeds or of rice. Each stands near a wide, shallow bowl, half filled with water. Standing with the back to the dish, the player carefully passes seeds over the left shoulder so that they fall into the water. These falling seeds form a pattern. The lover chants:

Hemp seed I sow,
Hemp seed will grow.
Let him who loves me
Come after me and mow.

The "sown" seeds give a hint or sign of the beloved's name or profession. If the seed pattern resembles a letter of the alphabet, then that is the first letter of the desired name. A pattern resembling a house suggests a wealthy suitor. A crown implies power, nobility, or royalty. An arrow stands for a hunter. A butter churn implies a dairy man or maid.

Country Superstition and Grand Idea   A truly reasonable person might see in the divination bowl only a heap of silly seeds. Divinations might seem ridiculous superstition. However, they represent a surprisingly important medieval idea. Everything within the universe is gloriously interrelated. Heavenly harmonies in the stars influence people's lives. Human destinies have their echos in the trees and plants, even the stones of the natural world. There are patterns common to the heavens, human beings, and the animal and plant kingdoms. The trained eye perceives these excellent designs. Divination is the opportunity for such a pattern to become "apparent" to a beholder.

Yarrow   Another Valentine divination is performed with the *yarrow* plant. The lovers assigned by lot each give to the other a small green yarrow sprig. Its vigor or death will predict faithfulness or faithlessness in love. If by the meal's end the yarrow is lively and fresh, then the love it represents will be true. Fading or wilting yarrow indicates wavering and waning interest in love.

Night Yarrow, Eringoes, and Pillow Faces Sometimes the yarrow faith test extends beyond the feast into Valentine's night. Five yarrow leaves are pinned to the sleeper's pillow and sprinkled with rosewater. The leaves' healthy survival till morning proves durability of the affection they represent. Withered or dead leaves in the morning spell love's doom.

Two more night divinations reveal the identity of the future beloved. *Eringoes* are leaves of the plant *eryngium*, or Sea Holly. It is used so often to foretell young people's love that the plant is also called "lad's love" or "boy love." The leaves placed at night inside the pillow are said to cause the beloved to appear in a dream to the sleeper.

This request must be repeated three times before falling asleep:

Good Valentine, be kind to me:
In dreams let me my true love see.

Another night-time revelation comes in the amusing guise of *pillow faces*. Several pillows filled with eryngium or a combination of divination herbs such as yarrow and rosemary are placed at the foot of the bed. By morning they twice reveal love. First, the herbs' aroma causes dreams of love. Second, the pillows themselves will have been creased, pushed, and disarranged. Looked at from afar, they reveal pillow faces: the outline of the beloved's facial features.

Valentine Conversations and Rebus Writing Valentining conversations at table should be about love. Since great affection is often thought mysteriously powerful, however, Valentine feasters often write Valentines in mysterious fashion. A *rebus* replaces a word. A rebus is a drawing of a person or idea or a thing. Each guest must write at least one message in rebus writing before the feast is over. For example:

(I   fear   you   will   leave   me.)

(My   heart   belongs   to   you.)

(You   are   beautiful.)

All of these Valentinings remind the celebrants that love is one of the most powerful emotions that human beings are capable of expressing. Though the month of February generally is still chill with winter's cold, it promises the spring to come. People as well as the animals of the natural world ought to rejoice in the new season of love. St. Valentine's Day is the time for exultation in this greatest natural passion.

CHAPTER IV

March: Easter

A<small>N</small> Easter festival hall is decorated with evergreenery, spring flowers, and, on one side, a huge golden disk representing the sun. On the opposite wall is an equally brilliant silvery moon. Medieval Easter is as variable as the sun and the phases of the moon. It is a moveable feast in terms of quality and in time. It is solemn yet jolly, pious yet irreverent, restrained yet full of frolic. Easter commemorates the most profound religious mysteries, and the simplest human urges toward light and warmth.

Easter almost never occurs on the same day twice. In fact, medieval Easter is not a day but an astonishing 120-day cycle of feasts and fasts. Easter Sunday is simply the central day. Easter begins nine weeks before Easter Sunday on the holiday called *Septuagesima*. Easter ends eight weeks after Easter Sunday on Trinity Day. Easter Sunday is moveable in the calendar. Sometimes it comes as early as March 22 or as late as April 23. Timing of Easter Sunday depends on the full moon of the spring equinox, March 21. Easter Sunday is the first Sunday after. Everything else in the 17-week Easter cycle is calculated forward or backward from that full moon day.

The sun is equally important at Easter. The holiday is named after the pagan Goddess of the Dawn and of Spring, Eostre. Easter rejoices in the sun's rising in the sky, bringing light and day. Easter especially revels in the ascending spring sun's warm triumph over the cold death of winter. Naturally, the Christian meanings of Easter fit perfectly. The Son's rising to Heaven brings the light of understanding and promises the day of salvation. His shining victory is over dark death.

Remarkable events in the 120-day Easter cycle take place in the churches. In homes and castles on each of these days particular foods and ceremonies are customary. But when Eleanor of Aquitaine came to England to be its Queen and an eager, learned courtier tried to explain all 120 days of local Easter customs at once, she stamped her delicate, determined foot and said, "Tell me what is particularly Easterly." The answer: *pace egging, morris dances*, and *mystery plays*.

Pace Egging Once the banquet guests are seated to the accompaniment of lively music, the Surveyor calls attention to the centerpiece on the high table. It is a large glass bowl, filled to the brim with gorgeously painted *pace eggs*. Pace eggs are hard-boiled eggs decorated with flower and vegetable dye paints. At their tapered ends are borders of lace, embroidery, and tiny glass jewels. Some are painted with each guest's family design: four gold lions are on a pace egg, colored half purple and half red; three black crescents surround a wheel on an egg dyed gold and bright blue. A baker's pace eggs have the symbol of a unicorn and a lion together propping up a pretzel.

Pace means Pasch, from the same Hebrew word as the Jewish holiday of Passover, and also means Easter. Beautiful pace eggs are gifts for performers who soon will come pace egging. They act a short play and beg coins and pace eggs for their labors. A popular pace-egging comedy is St. George and the Dragon, such as mummers perform on Twelfth Night.

Another type of pace egging is egg rolling. On a smooth carpet on the floor, two teams of guests compete to roll eggs in straight lines. Then they take turns rolling eggs through wickets; some, particularly fast; or especially slowly; or spinning; all, of course, without cracking.

An emperor and churchmen beneath a canopy, and the empress and nobles, below, march in a street procession led by torch-bearers.

Morris Dancers Easter foods and ciders are served, including roast lamb, apple fritters, and tansy cake, made with pleasantly sharp herbs. A fanfare sounds for silence in the hall. Suddenly, stamping steps and jingling bells signal the entrance of the *morris dancers.* Twelve dancers dressed in dark tights and tunics wear wooden clogs on their feet or wooden taps on their shoes. They have ankle bands with many small bells. Holly wreaths are on their heads. They carry tall straight canes with flowing scarves.

First they make a graceful, noisy procession around the hall, unfurling their scarves to stream behind them. Then, gathering to form a circle, they slowly, rhythmically move clockwise, following the path of the sun, with elaborate foot patterns. The musicians play vigorous music with cymbals, pipes, and tabor drums. The *morris dancers* stamp and jump high in the air.

Their name, morris, comes from the Moorish dancers of Spain. But their dances are traditional Spring rituals for fertility of the land. The insistent tapping steps and the bell ringings once were thought to awaken slumbering spirits of the fields. Leaping is a reminder to them to allow grain to grow high, flocks to multiply, and people to prosper.

Mystery Play of Noah's Flood More feast foods are followed by juggling, magic, miming, and music. Interrupting a quiet song, a tall man with white beard and dramatic loud voice announces:

I am God who the world has wrought,
Heaven and earth, and all of naught.
I see my people, in deed and thought,
Are set in foul sin.
I will destroy mankind!

This actor introduces the play called *The Deluge.* It is the story of Noah's Flood. Usually played outdoors on a moveable stage called a *pageant wagon,* it is a mystery play from the English town of Chester. Mystery plays dramatize popular Bible stories. They are meant to entertain as well as to teach. Their makers and players are town craftsmen whose work is suited to the tale. *The Deluge* is acted by the water carriers.

The actor called God summons faithful Noah, and instructs him to build the ark 300 cubits long, 50 wide, and 50 high. Noah's family must stock it with pairs of all the birds and beasts in the land so that after the flood all species of life will be able to be renewed. Noah's son Japhet gathers cats, dogs, otters, foxes, and hares. Noah's wife adds bears, wolves, apes, marmosets, weasels, and squirrels. When the rains come, the family itself must enter the ark. But Noah's wife refuses.

NOAH: Wife, come in! Why do you stand there?
Come in! It is time. I fear we will drown.

WIFE: Yea, Sir, set up your sail.
And row forth, with evil hail!
For without fail
I will not budge out of this town.
I have my friends here, everyone.
Not one of them will drown if I can save her life.
If you don't like it, Noah, get another wife!

[*She scolds and shouts. She drinks wine with her gossiping friends, refusing her husband, sons, and all advice. Only at the last moment, they drag her to the ark.*]

NOAH: Welcome, wife, to this boat!

The Deluge is closely related to the Easter themes of rebirth, renewal, and, after a time of death, resurrection of life in finer form.

Easter's Other Days Each day of the seventeen weeks of Easter has its own special symbolic *pax cakes*, pancakes, dances, contests, and games. A single modern Easter day is 120 times simpler than medieval Easter's cycle of Quinquegesima, Shrove Tuesday, Ash Wednesday, Mothering Sunday, Carling Sunday, Palm Sunday, Maundy Thursday, Good Friday, Rogation Sunday, Ascension, Pentecost, and Whit Monday. Each celebrates the miracle of the new day.

CHAPTER V

April: All Fool's Day

As guests file into the April banquet hall, trumpets start a magnificent fanfare but end it with a crashing of pan covers. Servitors wear their hats and costumes backward. Others carrying empty trays walk backward. Standing near the high table is a man dressed in black wearing a tall pointed hat adorned with figures of stars and the moon. He snatches flames from the air. He discovers butterflies in his sleeve. He makes the dog sing. A chain's locked links spring apart at his touch. This magician saws a beautiful young woman in two.

The April world is upside down. Things are not what they seem. Elegant order is turned topsy-turvy. The results are hilarious. All Fool's Day is a splendid celebration of the ridiculous.

The Lord of Misrule, Motley, and Whiddershins Instead of a noble lord or lady presiding at the high table, the chair of honor is reserved for the jester. He is the Lord of Misrule. Dressed in a fool's costume of many colors, called *motley*, he wears a long, floppy, pointed hat with bells at its tip. He carries a sceptor topped with a small head, which also wears a belled fool's cap.

Servitors perform their jobs backward. The least important tables are served first, the high table last. Bows are not made toward people but away from them. People write notes in mirror writing, starting at the right side of the page with letters moving left. The Surveyor's announcements are reversed: "Fanfare a play will now musicians!" he solemnly declares. The festivities all take place in reverse order, which is called *whiddershins*.

The Feast of Fools and the Boy Bishop   All Fool's Day is often joined to a church holiday called the Feast of Fools. In churches, monasteries, and schools, students control the teachers, and the young rule the old. There are boy bishops. Holy services are recited whiddershins in this April (or January) feast.

Adults play with children's mechanical toys; children mock the elders and order them around.

Feast of Asses and Balaam's Ass A celebration called the Feast of Asses—its proper Latin title is *Festum Asinorum*—is particularly popular in the French towns of Rouen and Beauvais. Short plays depict the adventures of the Bible prophet Balaam and his wondrous donkey. An evil king asks Balaam to prophesy for a fee, and curse the children of Israel. Instead, Balaam blesses them. Later, however, when he foolishly disregards certain instructions God has given him, his ass obeys them. Balaam's ass becomes protector of the prophet. The rider is directed by the mount. The ass wisely speaks to the foolish prophet who will not hear.

Mirror of Fools and Brunellus the Ass Other asses teach and preach on All Fool's Day. Interspersed among excellent feast foods and entertainments, asinine tales are read or acted out from a brilliantly funny twelfth-century book called the *Mirror of Fools*. Nigel Wireker wrote it about a very special university student at Salerno and Paris, who is a donkey named Brunellus the Ass. He leaves the farm world because he is annoyed that his tail is too short. In his ass world, cattle talk, turtles fly, oxen are harnessed *behind* the carts, donkeys give lute concerts, and bold rabbits threaten fearful lions.

Everyone at the feast tries to tell a ridiculous story and get a listener to believe it. A famous tale, for example, describes the adventures of Eve's mother.

April's Revelry Revealed There is sense to all this nonsense. All Fool's Day reminds merrymakers that rules are sometimes uncomfortable for us to follow but disorder is disastrous. Things may seem difficult, but if the world were turned upside down, they would be even worse. After the ludicrous amusements of All Fool's Day, people willingly turn their attentions forward and deal with the restraints of life right side up.

CHAPTER VI

May: Mayday

MARVELOUS Mayday's customs and costumes, decorations and dances, and delectable green foods signal the change of season. Many Mayday rituals are remembrances of pagan attempts to force Spring to return to the world. Dancers stamp the ground to reawaken it, and shrill May horns, loud May whistles, and tinkling May bells alert sleeping spirits of fields and forests to the changing seasons. At the center of revelry is the Maypole. It is a tall, strong shaft, crowned with garlands of leaves and flowers, and wound round with brightly colored ribbons. It resembles a giant tree. Near it, the Queen of the May is crowned. Around it, she leads circle dances. The Maypole contest games identify the strongest, tallest, swiftest, prettiest, bravest, smallest, loudest, and best. These Mayday champions place small bells on the Maypole. Ringings and ceremonies encourage the "guardian of trees" to create abundance.

Maypoles Many towns and cities have Maypoles so tall and heavy. (some rise ninety feet high in the air) they must be anchored deeply in the ground. These poles remain standing throughout the year. Only on Mayday are they decorated with their flower crowns, ribbons, and streamers. In London, the Maypole gives its name to the neighborhood, Mayfair. The fine old London church with the odd name of St. Andrew Undershaft stands small beneath a Mayshaft.

Smaller Maypoles are set up for Maydays and taken down between. They are placed where space is large enough for dancing and festivity, outdoors or indoors. In a banquet hall, a Maypole erected with a wide, stable base and reinforced with bricks or stones is a fine centerpoint for the merriment.

Wreaths and Hoops in the Hall The door to the house or hall is decorated with a May wreath; so are some windows. A May wreath's circular arrangement of evergreen boughs, like the modern Christmas wreath, announces the joyous season to all who see it.

Large hoops used in the game of hoop rolling are decorated on their inner rims. Green ribbons and small bells, evenly spaced, are arranged so that when the hoops are rolled there are flashes of color and jingling sounds. Sometimes hoops are suspended by attractive ropes and chains from the ceiling, turning and tinkling as air and people move in the hall.

Wreaths and Baldrics for May Guests Mayday guests also are wreathed. Each wears a crown of green leaves with flowers, pinned to the hair or attached to a well-fitting skullcap. Another costume decoration is a green *baldric*. This is a long ribbon placed over the right shoulder to cross the chest and the back diagonally, finally to tie at the left hip.

The Queen of the May A fanfare introduces the Surveyor's crowning of the Queen of the May. She may be the prettiest or youngest or tallest or most honored guest. No matter how she is chosen, the queen must represent a particular quality in the superlative. Wearing a golden crown with a single gold leaf at her forehead, she announces the May games and awards prizes to the winners. Along with the usual fabulous feast entertainments, such as juggling and magic, May games alternate with foods and drinks, which on Mayday are all colored spring green.

Gardeners carefully plant and tend spring vegetable and fruit plots while two men talk and a woman sews.

Spring Green Foods and Jack-in-the-Green The trenchers are delicately green parsley bread slices. On these, green salads with lettuce, spinach, peas, endive, fennel, and green gage plum are served, followed by a light green apple cider. A Mayday favorite is fruited beef and green peppermint rice. Apple slices are dipped in minted green whipped cream. Four guests share a small cream bowl, usually leaf-shaped. A delectable desert is *Jack-in-the-Green*. Each guest is served a large gingerbread-man cookie called Jack-in-the-Green or Jack-in-the-Bush. On his head is a May wreath of green sprinkles or small sprigs of parsley or bright green lime icing.

Maying-Round-the-Merry-Maypole Guests join hands in a circle around the Maypole. Moving clockwise, they circle it, dancing, stamping, and acting a set of ancient May rituals. The melody is the familiar circle game "Here We Go Round the Mulberry Bush." Each stanza demonstrates a special custom accompanied by suitable antics. The circle of hand-clasped guests sings:

Here we go round the merry Maypole
The merry Maypole, the merry Maypole,
Here we go round the merry Maypole
On a cold and frosty May morning!

The dancers stop the circle, drop hands, and *collect the May.* Mayday festivities in the country begin before dawn. Young men and women go to the forests and fields to collect evergreen boughs and meadow flowers. These become the wreaths and decorations for the hall, guests, and the Maypole. Greenery and flowers together are called "the May." *Going-a-Maying* is the name of this early morning woodland party. The first verse's gestures imitate bending to pick flowers, and reaching to cut branches.

This is the way we collect the May . . .
On a cold and frosty May morning.

Next *we gather May dew.* The early May morning dew on the grasses and mosses is said to be both lucky and healthy. Rubbed onto the skin, the pure water is thought to create a wonderful complexion. Third, *we stamp for Spring,* each dancer lifting the right knee high in the air and stamping the foot down hard, again and again. Next *we bake Jack-in-the-Green,* stirring dough and cutting out the gingerbread-man. And *we Morris Dance.* Each dancer flourishes a flowing scarf and twirls round rhythmically.

Superlative Games While on other holidays, participation in games is more important than winning them, on Mayday, competition is their purpose. In ancient Celtic spring rites, the gods were thought to listen best to requests from those they already blessed with superlative abilities. "The best" petitioned for all. Therefore the Queen of the May directs the games determining the fastest race, longest leap, farthest throw of a ball, longest-held note, most skillful hoop roll, most accurate ring-toss, best guess of number of beans in a barrel, and finest archer.

Guests, watching, blow horns and whistles to cheer their champions. To each winner, the Queen of the May gives a small set of bells on an ankle band. The winner wears it briefly. Before the May games are done, he or she cavorts round the Maypole, jingling loudly, removes the bell band, and places it on one of the Maypole's several small hooks for such trophy gifts.

Backgammon, Chess, and Billiards Board games, such as backgammon and chess, are played on Mayday. Sometimes these are quiet, private table games. Otherwise they are elaborate spectacles with the floor designed as a game board and costumed people acting as "pieces": the chess king, queen, or rook.

Billiards, or pool, also is a Mayday pleasure. Players use a billiard table with cues or an indoor or outdoor floor court arranged for teams.

Nine Man's Morris One of the most popular pastimes is Nine Man's Morris. Noblemen or shepherds play indoors or outside on a small well-carved board or roughly cut grass or dirt court. The basic Nine Man's Morris pattern gives each player nine counters, identifiable by color or shape as his or her own. They can be ivory or wood balls, carved and enameled, or crude sticks or stones. Counters are called *morrells*, another name for the game itself. The object is to get three morrells in a straight row. The player making such a line has the privilege of taking any one morrell from his opponent. The player collecting the most morrells wins Nine Man's Morris. Two types of boards are:

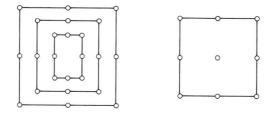

The holes receive the morrells. When played outdoors, on a "lifesize" board with people as "counters," the movements of the players resemble a morris dance. The game's name comes from that or from the nine morrells.

Mayday's Other Seasonal Delights   Mayday's other festivities are traditional fabulous feast entertainments, especially similar to June's Midsummer customs.

CHAPTER VII

June: Midsummer Eve

DURING a Midsummer Eve ceremony, people in a candlelight procession chant this riddle:

Green is Gold.
Fire is Wet.
Future's Told.
Dragon's Met.

Actually, this riddle-chant contains four hidden questions. When is the color green truly gold? When is fire wet? When is the future foretold? When is a dragon met? To all the answer is: On Midsummer Eve!

This holiday's ceremonies are seldom what they seem. Even the name Midsummer is a surprise because the holiday is celebrated not in the middle of summertime but at its beginning. It commemorates the summer solstice, when the sun seems to stand still and the year's days are longest and nights shortest. Midsummer festivities honor the earth's awakening after the winter's sleep, as in the Mayday festival. These particular spring and summer holidays celebrate the earth's creation of the young new leaves and grasses. These earliest greens look golden. Therefore, Nature's first green is gold.

A second hidden question in the Midsummer riddle is harder to answer. Water cannot burn nor fire flame in water. However,

Midsummer fire is wet because it is customary to float lighted candles or torches on water. These flames accompany wishes for the future. If a small candle-boat safely sails from shore to shore of a pond, then the wish it represents will be fulfilled. Festival fires on the waters are thought to announce desires and foretell the future.

Other Midsummer ceremonies are also diviners of destiny. One is *St. John's bread*, which is not a bread at all, but a delicious sweet, dried fruit.

Other vegetable fortune tellers, such as the plant called *St. John's wort*, are named for St. John the Baptist, the Christian saint whose birthday is on Midsummer Day. Midsummer Eve therefore also is called St. John's Eve.

This holiday's curious customs, however, are graced by a dramatic beast that has little to do with St. John. A Midsummer reveler enacting the role of St. George must "kill" a huge "dragon," whether it is a dragon-shaped kite, or a gigantic pastry dragon subtletie.

Merrily mixing customs of ancient pagan sun-worship with medieval Christian lore, Midsummer Eve is that remarkable time when:

Green is Gold.
Fire is Wet.
Fortune's Told.
Dragon's Met.

Festival Fires   June's end is a fine time for outdoor celebrations. Midsummer fires and water fortune-tellings are more usual under the evening sky than in a hall. But when rain requires the shelter of a roof, indoor festivities can be equally vibrant.

All Midsummer entertainments revolve around the *festival fire*. Outside it is an open bonfire, usually made of lighted logs. The bonfire originally was fueled by animal bones. In fact, the name for the festive flames originally was "bone fire." Sometimes it is called *Beltane fire*. That name refers to the Druid fires thousands of years ago honoring the pagan god Bal or Bel.

If a bonfire outdoors is not possible, a candle circle on the hall floor is a fine alternative. Twenty-four candles in sturdy holders are arranged in a ring with much space about them for guests to march and dance.

Everyone entering the festival space and walking from ceremony to seat always must circle the fire clockwise. This imitates the path of the sun, rising in the east and setting in the west.

Crowns and Boughs   Each Midsummer Eve celebrant wears a birch wreath crowning the head, or a garland made of small-leaved branches, or a sprig of new green leaves pinned to the costume on the left side, over the heart.

First Rogation   At a sign from the Surveyor, a fanfare signals the beginning of the ceremonies. Guests gather in a broad circle around the fire. Joining hands, they slowly, rhythmically, move clockwise, chanting the Midsummer riddle seven times:

Green is Gold.
Fire is Wet.
Fortune's Told.
Dragon's Met.

This is the first *rogation*, a circular procession that begins and ends the festivities. After the seventh circling, the person assigned to be the "head" drops hands with the "tail" and leads a serpentine procession away from the fire. All guests are seated.

St. John's Humney   The Surveyor presents the customary welcome wassail and other banquet ceremonies, as at every proper medieval fabulous feast.

Before the service of the first course, however, a fanfare announces *St. John's Humney*. Every guest performs this counting game, which predicts the answer to a question beginning with "How many?" How many years until I—? How many months—? How many people—? How many hours—? How many feathers—? How many circles—? Each guest thinks of a question and then obtains the answer by biting into and eating the *St. John's bread*, carefully removing the seeds and then counting them. The number of St. John's bread seeds reveals how many, or *humney*.

St. John's bread is the graceful, long, brown, delectably sweet seedpod from the locust tree. Also called carob, it tastes delightfully similar to cocoa or chocolate. Its flat seeds are so perfectly regular in shape, size, and weight that carob seed has been a measure for precious metals and jewels. The weight of twenty-four carat gold or the size of a four carat diamond originally was determined by St. John's bread, carob seed. The name carats is derived from carobs. St. John's bread itself is named for a legend that St. John, alone without food in the desert, kept himself healthy by eating locust seedpods, his bread of life.

Cuckoo-Foot Ale   No matter what beautiful foods are selected for the Midsummer feast, at least one course must be accompanied by *cuckoo-foot ale*. This carbonated drink spiced with ginger, anise, and basil celebrates the cuckoo bird. Its song is sure proof of the spring and summer seasons. A musician imitates a cuckoo sound on a recorder or trumpet. Then guests raise their glasses to toast the bird and nature's season of rebirth and regeneration.

The Cuckoo Song   Cuckoo-foot ale is best drunk to the lively sounds of the *cuckoo song* called "Summer is a-coming in." This popular round performed by musicians and guests is one of the oldest English songs. It reminds people to rejoice in their senses in the summer season.

Summer is a-coming in.
Loudly sing, cuckoo!
The seed grows,

Fishermen with line and net, fowlers (one with a crossbow), and an animal herder collect spring feast food.

The meadow blows,
And the woods spring anew.
Sing, cuckoo!
Ewe bleats after lamb,
Cow lows after calf;
Bullock leaps,
Buck starts.
Merrily sing, cuckoo!
Cuckoo! Cuckoo!
Well do you sing, cuckoo!
Never cease singing now.

Diviner Eggs and Destiny Cakes Two Midsummer feast necessities are *diviner eggs* and *destiny cakes*. Both are thought to "show" the future by a shape or a sign in a food.

Every guest is given a small glass cup or a bowl with an unbroken raw egg. Carefully cracking the egg, the feaster pours it into the cup and "reads" the shape. Does it look like a house? The family may soon move. Is it a hat? A student may soon graduate. Is it a trunk suggesting travel? Or a tree? Or a shovel? Something in the near future is thought to be discovered or divined. Then a servitor carrying a large bowl requests that each diviner egg be poured into that common bowl. Thereafter, while other courses are being served, the Chief Cook prepares *almoundyn eyroun*, a superb omelet with almonds, raisins, honey, and spices.

This is later presented with another Midsummer divination food, *destiny cakes*. Prepared beforehand, they are served from a platter completely covered with a decorative cloth. The feaster reaches under to select an amusingly shaped cake. Like the diviner egg, it predicts the future. The destiny cake may resemble a letter of the alphabet or an animal or a building or a cart. Whatever, the cake's shape may be made by the baker but it is interpreted by the imagination of the beholder. Feasters "reading" the egg and the cake learn a detailed story of the future.

Midsummer Rose The *Midsummer rose* helps to distinguish between true love and no love. The feaster takes a rose from a vase on the table and plucks a petal, and says "He (or she) loves me." Working clockwise, the next petal plucked means "He (or she) loves me not." The Midsummer rose petals fall one by one; each is sign of affection or none. The last petal tells the tale of glee or gloom.

St. John's Wort and Hemp Seed To test whether love will endure, each guest is given a fragrant, leafy branch of the plant called *St. John's wort*. Just like the St. Valentine's divination with yarrow, if the leaves do not wilt by the feast's end, then the love is durable. If St. John's wort is taken home overnight and remains fresh in the morning, love will be vigorous and long-lasting. A droopy, dying, or dead St. John's wort predicts a short, bleak romance. Another Valentining game popular at Midsummer is the Hemp Seed toss.

Wet Fire In none of these Midsummer prediction games do the players tell their own wishes. Each guest simply reads the message of the St. John's Humney or the diviner eggs and destiny cakes or the Midsummer rose or the St. John's wort or the hemp seed. The *wet fire* ritual, however, allows the Midsummer player the chance not only to foretell but to help to compel the future.

Outdoors, near a pond or pool, or indoors, near a large, water-filled tub in the hall, each guest lights a candle. It is securely set in a stiff paper "boat" and floated on the water. Sometimes a silent wish is made before setting the flame on the water, or a short message is written on a scrap of paper placed in the boat, or the wish is inscribed inside the boat itself. Candle and wish then voyage together. Fires on the water that safely reach the opposite side of the pool show promise that the wishes will come true. A wind-snuffed flame or a drowned boat-wish is a sad omen.

Sometimes a seacoast town will cast floating torches and bonfires on its waters at Midsummer. It does so to insure good luck for the coming year for all the townspeople.

"Old" Pagan Customs and "New" Medieval Uses No matter how old or young, people joyously yet seriously join Midsummer games. Few remember who first taught particular rituals. Even fewer people know why they are performed or what they mean. As with many holiday festivities they are simply beautiful "traditions." They please those who perform them. Year after year they are passed from oldster to child, and so from century to century.

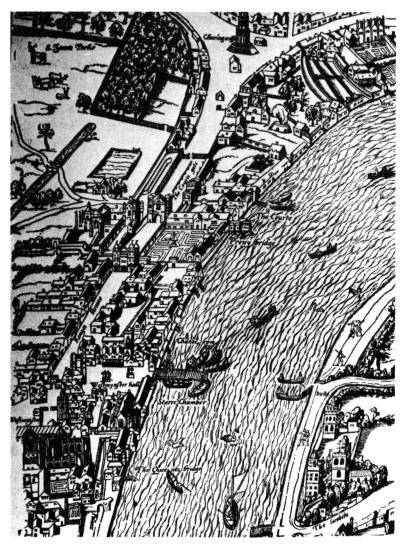

Easily accessible by wharves and stairs, London's River Thames is a major thoroughfare for commerce, travel, and "wet fire."

It is astonishing that the same fire customs serving an ancient pagan sun god are rededicated to the Christian St. John. However, that is a clever idea of many "new" beliefs: to take what is useful in the old and make it serve the new. Pope Gregory and St. Augustine agreed that what people enjoyed in their earlier faith could be turned to advantage for Christianity.

St. John's Fern   Even scientific minds, who otherwise might reject magic and marvels as simply silly, sometimes follow "irrational" traditional ideas. Medieval physicians and churchmen oftentimes encourage people to look for *St. John's fern.* It is better than medication to change the mood. It is more effective than prayers to remove nasty responsibilities. St. John's fern allows total escape from unpleasantness by giving immediate invisibility! The finder and keeper of this delicate plant spore simply disappears at will and reappears at desire. That, at least, is the legend which inspires the quest for it. While reasonable people may not expect the impossible, nevertheless, they secretly wish for it. St. John's fern dramatizes that hope.

Midsummer Mumming Plays   Many a nobleman keeps workers and craftsmen on his staff primarily because they are skillful in celebrations. The wealthy Sir John Paston complains in a letter that his groom may not be great with the animals but is a wonderful actor of Robin Hood and St. George. Entertaining at Midsummer feasts in town, cottage, or castle, costumed players such as Sir John Paston's groom present traditional mummings, the short dramas that have no suspense and no surprise ending but characters amusingly familiar. Mummings please because they are traditional ritual, age-old humor, and simple, good theater. Like the Twelfth Night mummings of January, the favorite Midsummer mumming hero is St. George, the patron saint of England.

A Play of St. George   Although Midsummer Day is St. John's birthday, the Midsummer adventures of St. George usually have this cast of characters:

1. the Kind King
2. the Beautiful Princess
3. the Red Dragon
4. Noble St. George
5. the Old Doctor

[*A fierce Dragon has been terrorizing a kingdom. The only way to please the beast and keep it from destroying the land is to feed it plump cattle. But when there are no more animals, it accepts young boys and girls as sacrificial offerings. At last, the King must offer his own child. He loves his daughter, the Princess, more than his life. He laments:*]

KING: Woe is me, my darling daughter,
That I must live and see your slaughter.

[*Bravely she receives his blessing, and, dressed as a bride, goes to the swamp to await her death by the Dragon. St. George happens to ride by. He sees the beautiful Princess. Hearing her story, he insists on trying to help her. But the maiden, who has immediately fallen in love with him, tries to convince him to leave her. She fears he, too, will be killed.*]

PRINCESS: Good youth, good sir, spur on your horse
And fly to take another course.
The Dragon—foul and fierce and sly—
Will grind his jaws to make me die.
I beg of you, be off in haste!

ST. GEORGE: For you to die would be a waste!
I will not take one step from here
Until I rescue you from fear.
My horse, my cross, my sword, and I
Will bring this monster forth to die.

[*Suddenly, the gigantic Dragon roars. It attacks the Princess, the King, and St. George. It also menaces the King's subjects, who are the audience. Sometimes this Dragon is an actor in an elaborate costume, or it is a giant kite on poles or strings, flown over the heads of the feasters, while an actor shouts his lines off-stage. Sometimes it is a huge, dragon-shaped sugar, marzipan, or pastry subtletie that stands on a platform while an acrobatic player speaks his threats.*]

DRAGON: Stand on head, stand on feet!
　　Meat, meat, meat, for me to eat!
　　I am the Dragon. Here are my jaws!
　　I am the Dragon. Here are my claws!
　　Meat, meat, meat, for me to eat.
　　Stand on my head, stand on my feet!

[*Somersaulting and lunging, the Dragon terrifies everyone, except St. George. George boldly rushes at him
with his sword and cross. The Dragon quietly grovels
at his feet. St. George directs the Princess to control
the monster.*]

ST. GEORGE: Now place your belt around his neck.
　　Tame as a dog, he will not harm a speck.

[*They walk proudly. When the belt accidentally slips
from the Dragon's head, it turns again to attack. It is more
cruel than before. This time, St. George drives his sword
through the Dragon's body. But not before the beast had
killed the Princess and the King, and seriously wounded
St. George.*

　*Into this scene of death and destruction jauntily walks
the Old Doctor:*]

OLD DOCTOR: I am the Doctor, and I cure all ills.
　　Just gulp my potions, and swallow my pills.
　　I can cure the itch, the stitch,
　　The pox, the palsey, and the gout.
　　All pains within, all pains without.

[*He stands over the King and the Princess. Holding
above their heads two large pills, he says:*]

OLD DOCTOR: Get up, good King! Get up, his Daughter!
　　You are too good to end in slaughter.

[*Once the Doctor puts pills in their mouths, they rise
up at once. The Doctor now moves to St. George:*]

OLD DOCTOR: Get up, St. George, old England's knight.
　　You wounded the Dragon. I'll finish the fight.

[Taking the magic pill, St. George also leaps up hale and healthy. Now the Doctor forces a huge pill down the Dragon's throat. It roars loudly. It flails and fumes. It threatens and thrashes, thuds and dies.]

Saint George and the dragon decorate an elaborate capital "L" from a 15th century French printer's alphabet.

The Play Finale   The actors all bow and collect coins as thanks for their performance. If this Midsummer dragon has been an edible subtletie, then the Surveyor directs the serving of its pieces to the feasters. If the dragon has been a player or a kite, then all feasters are served dragon-shaped cakes or sweet, carob-scented, triangular cookies called *St. John's dragon-wings.*

Farewell Rogation and Threading the Needle   A procession closes the Midsummer festival. Guests all take candles or hold their decorative wreaths or small green boughs in hand. They perform the farewell rogation round the bonfire or round the hall. Moving in line in a circle, clockwise, they chant the Midsummer riddle seven times to assure the chance to do the same next year.

The person called the "head" once again drops hands with the "tail" and leads a procession dance called *Threading the Needle*. Two people (or several pairs) are assigned to break away from the line. Facing one another near the exit to the festival space, with hands raised and meeting to form a pointed arch, they make the Needle's Eye. The long serpentine line passing through their arch is the Thread. Having threaded the needle that sews yearly traditions to life, the revelers leave. Midsummer proves magnificently that:

Green is Gold.
Fire is Wet.
Fortune's Told.
Dragon's Met.

July: St. Swithin's Day

JULY'S festivities borrow customs from other months, particularly May and June. But instead of welcoming the new season, July celebrates Summer's abundance of fruits, vegetables, pleasures of the outdoors—and rain. A charming weather holiday, particularly in England, is St. Swithin's Day. Rain on St. Swithin's Day is said to predict rain for forty days afterward. A dry St. Swithin's Day means drought for the next forty days. Apples watered by St. Swithin's Day rain become the most luscious. July foods, rituals, and games are associated with the season's weather.

St. Swithin's Legend   Legend tells that pious old Bishop Swithin of Winchester in the ninth century asked that when he died his body be buried in a simple grave in the churchyard. One hundred years later, people wanted to honor his memory by making a beautiful tomb. They moved his bones to the elaborate new resting place. Constant rain fell. People thought the rain represented St. Swithin's tears of displeasure. They again moved his bones to a fine spot inside Winchester Cathedral. The rains stopped. The Saint's spirit's sorrow turned to joy, and the sky shone brightly. Ever after, St. Swithin's Day rain was thought a predictor of weather to come.

Country folk chant a rhyme that goes like this:

Three bishops stand before the altar, one carrying a reliquary; other churchmen (one with glasses) sing from a hymnbook.

St. Swithin's Day, if it does rain
For forty days it will remain!
St. Swithin's Day, if it is fair
For forty days it will rain *na mair* (no more).

Medieval scientists, however, use meteorological instruments as astrolabes to calculate likely weather changes. Taking sun and star measurements on St. Swithin's Day, they make the weather almanacs that people use throughout the year. These help determine proper time for planting gardens, harvesting crops, and traveling.

Apples for Eating and for Bobbing   Large apples are polished and cut in half horizontally. The seeds appear to be arranged in a star shape called a pentangle. Its five-sided continuous design represents the perfection of the year's cycle of seasons. They seem never beginning and never ending. Guests eat as many apples as supply and desire allow. Before it is eaten, however, one half of each apple must be dipped in a bowl of salt water, shared by every five guests. The water is remembrance of St. Swithin's tears. The other half of the apple is dipped in golden whipped cream, spiced and tinted by saffron or dandelion. Every five guests share a bowl. Gold, like the apple's pentangle, represents timelessness. Never tarnishing, never changing, gold seems perfect and eternal. Eating such symbolic foods is a wish for long life.

Apple bobbing is often hilarious. Apples are floated on the surface of a large tub filled with water. Guests kneel around the tub with their hands clasped behind their backs. Each guest must take an apple by bobbing: leaning forward for a piece of fruit by grabbing it with his or her teeth. Since teeth are not as flexible as fingers, many a confident bobber is surprised by an unexpected dunking. Each guest bobs until securing one apple.

Other July Festivities   July's summer games and rites resemble those of winter and of spring. Circle games and races often take place near a Maypole, reminding revelers of the spring just passed. And when they eat such treats as plum and currant bread, they look forward to August's High Summer festival on *Lammas Day.*

CHAPTER IX

August: Lammas Day

AUGUST is bread time. Bakers give lessons in geometry by baking round breads, square breads, ovals, rectangles, trapezoids, and figure eights. The rainbow's colors are mixed with delicious fragrances in red rose-petal bread, golden-orange saffron loaves, yellow lemon bread, green parsley bread, blue thistle bread, indigo plum bread, and purple violet bread. Whimsical animal breads represent monkeys, elephants, and dragons. Architectural bread sculptures are castles and multi-decked warships. Special molded breads depict Eve in the Garden of Eden or Roman noblemen or a king of a foreign land. Celestial breads are stars, sun, moon, and a mechanical clock showing the planets in orbit. And almost every bake shop or street vendor sells pretzels, some salty, some sweet with raisins and glazed with honey. Breads honor Lammas Day, (Lammas means "loaf mass") and it is marked by a church celebration blessing grains and breads, and offering thanks to God for a good harvest.

Lammas Day entertainments are typical feast fare. But the muffins, buns, pies, and breads signal the high point of the summer growing season. Spring's promise is fulfilled. August is called High Summer or *Hohsum.* Soon after, the agricultural year descends to its end.

Lammas Lands   In the country and towns, fields for growing grains and crops are usually fenced to keep animals out. Otherwise

73

From her streetcorner table, a baker sells conical loaves and pretzels; another bakes breads in a portable oven.

they might trample or eat the harvest. On Lammas Day, the gates of certain fields are opened. Sheep and other animals are allowed to graze these Lammas Lands. Honoring this free pasturage, Lammas feasts are held in townhouse, country cottage, and noble castle.

Lammas Feasts Breads are important to the feast decorations and the menu. Tremendous bread and pastry subtleties are paraded through the hall. Throughout most of the meal they are displayed prominently. A bread castle, for example, is raised on a platform in the middle of the room, its colors and turrets admired until feast's end, when it is eaten.

Courses are served on bread or the courses themselves consist of types of bread, such as currant buns, shortbread, gingerbread, cucumber bread, and plum bread.

A favorite Lammas drink is Lamb's Wool, the splendid warm spiced cider with frothy baked apples floating on top.

Bringing Home the Bacon A humorous playlet reminds Lammas feasters that true love is hard work. According to custom, thought old even in the fourteenth century, a prize is offered to any couple who, after a year and a day of marriage, can swear truly that they have not regretted their wedding in any way at any time. The winners' reward is half a pig. For those enjoying pork and bacon, this is a valuable food gift. However, first the couple must *prove* their worthiness.

At Lammas festivals, a mock trial presents couples hoping to "bring home the bacon." Several sets of two guests, a man playing the Husband, and a woman playing the Wife, stand before a group of twelve guests, making up the Jury. A Judge, usually the Surveyor of the feast hall, presides. He asks questions of each Husband and Wife. He presents amusing absurdities beginning with "What if . . ." and ending each description of a domestic catastrophe with the question, "Was there no jealousy, joylessness, or jangling?" (This comes from a famous fourteenth century poem called *Piers Plowman*—*jangling* means loud complaining.) Since the couple is competing for perfect harmony in love, the Husband and Wife must create an answer that turns the adversity, humorously, into opportunity.

"What if," the Judge asks, "your husband chased the dog into the banquet hall, which spooked the cat, which leapt into the bowl of cream, which splashed the guest of honor? Was there no jealousy, joylessness, or jangling?" The Wife must immediately create an ingenious answer to prove her gladness that her wonderful husband caused this fortunate event!

Several eager couples compete in answering the Judge's questions before the Jury decides the verdict. The pair deemed worthy to "bring home the bacon" is the finest set of imaginative liars.

High Summer Finale The last event in the Lammas Feast is a candlelight procession around the hall. Everyone has a small loaf of bread with a candle set into it. When the lights are lit, the guests form a line to circle around the hall three times. The Surveyor then leads the celebrants through the door to go home. Each holds the bread that will be eaten the following day, with the exception of one quarter of it. That will be carefully preserved until next Lammas Day. After a year's new mornings, the Lammas quarter loaf will be made into crumbs to feed the birds. Then a new bread festival will begin.

CHAPTER X

September: Michaelmas

AFTER St. George, the second most famous dragon fighter is St. Michael. His adventures appear in the Bible. Michaelmas is the holiday honoring him. Churches and monasteries are named after him, such as the magnificent Mont Saint-Michel in France. In England, the fall season is called Michaelmas. People paying rent for a house or land four times a year call the autumn quarter the Michaelmas rent. Schools and universities name their autumn term Michaelmas. Even the September moon or harvest moon is also the Michaelmas moon. The best pleasures of Michaelmas, however, are the holiday itself. It is celebrated with three Gs: glove, goose, and ginger.

Glove, Fairs, and Pie Powder Court Every September, a gigantic glove is suspended from a pole on the roof of an important town building. It looks like the hand of a giant. Ten feet tall and made of leather with cotton or wood chips stuffing the fingers and thumb, the glove signals that a Michaelmas fair will begin.

Merchants come from miles around and from foreign countries. They pack beautiful fabrics, glassware, jewelry, and wines. Local craftsmen bring saddles, swords, and fireplace tongs. Weavers display tapestries. Potters purvey pitchers and platters. Farmers cart wheels of cheese and fresh vegetables. Horse breeders show ponies for sale.

The fair is a gala market. Every seller has a booth. These are neatly arranged around the borders of a field or in rows in a large hall. Musicians and acrobats entertain. Candy sellers shout to advertise their sweet wares. Customers come to buy and to be pleased.

Michaelmas fairs attract so many thousands of people that a special court is set up to hold trials for those who break market laws. Pie Powder Court is its surprising name. It means dusty feet court (powder foot, *pied poudre*, in French) because people traveling long on the highway to reach the fair have dusty, dirty boots.

The glove implies that the king, local nobleman, or town mayor gives permission for the market to welcome all sellers and all buyers. The glove stands for the handshake of promises. The king pledges to allow the fair and to provide the place and the money to announce it. The merchants and fair managers swear to give part of the profits to a worthy charity. (In just this way, English King John in 1211 granted the town of Sturbridge its charter for a fair, which helped support a hospital for lepers.) The glove also signifies open-handedness and generosity.

A Michaelmas glove is used to announce even small crafts fairs held indoors. Miniature markets are part of the entertainment of a Michaelmas feast. A fanciful glove brightly painted and set with imitation jewels is hung high on a wall or from the ceiling. Under the glove, guests delight in the second of the three Michaelmas Gs, the goose.

Goose Procession Whatever other feast foods are served, Michaelmas menus traditionally feature roast goose. If the cook is particularly skillful, the bird will have been skinned, stuffed, cooked, and then carefully refeathered so as to look alive. Brought to table with great ceremony on a platter decorated with autumn's fruits and flowers, the goose is carved with a special flourish. The neck is reserved for the most honored.

At a town market a fur-caped man buys a bull; others, behind, carry produce in a back basket and pick fruit for sale.

Those who cannot get a goose or who dislike its taste disguise a roast chicken with grey goose feathers. Or they create a goose subtletie with pastry and marzipan. A Michaelmas feast must have its proud bird for ceremonial procession, and every guest must taste it, for the belief is whoever eats goose on Michaelmas will not lack luck throughout the year.

Ginger Ginger accompanies other splendid feast dishes. Alternating with simpler foods are ginger ale, ginger beer, and ginger wine. There are gingerbread, ginger snaps, and ginger cake. Fish is baked with ginger. A fine ginger desert is *chardwardon*, made with large succulent wardon pears, sugar, cinnamon, nutmeg, and ginger. Ginger caramels served with curls of ginger root shavings conclude the feast.

No one knows for sure just why ginger is important at Michaelmas. Medieval physicians usually consider ginger a healing herb good for stomach and chest illnesses and for protection against infection. Just as St. Michael is said to be a guardian and healer, so the ginger plant with similar qualities ought to be remembered when he is. Others believe that fresh ginger is at its plentiful best in Europe in September. Another theory concerns a rich twelfth-century merchant who had a huge boatload of ginger brought from the East to sell at an English Michaelmas fair. He refused to pay a nasty new high tax to the town. Instead, he broke open his crates, hired jugglers, trumpeters, minstrels, and puppeteers to entertain while he gave away ginger to anyone who asked. Everyone did. Each gift was plenty for a year's worth of delicacies. Since that Michaelmas was so full of vim, vigor, and ginger, so the September feast was spiced with it ever after.

CHAPTER XI

October: Halloween

To celebrate Halloween is to roll pleasures of every other month into one. Halloween's customs are so familiar from other holidays it seems as if a conductor-composer of a great folk symphony summoned all the best musical themes to return for a grand finale. In fact, Halloween is the end of the year in the ancient pagan Celtic calendar. October's end is also called Summer's End, *Samhain*. So this festival allows the enjoyment one last time of bonfires, foods, and games of Mayday and June's Midsummer Eve. As the holiday signaling entrance to winter, Halloween also has a preview of its customs, as performance of the Twelfth Night play of St. George. October is the time when ghosts, spirits, witches, and supernatural beings are thought most powerful and most lonely. More Halloween divinations ask spirits questions about love and life than on all other holidays together.

Supernatural beings also are important in traditional Christian beliefs about October. Halloween is the evening before All Hallows or All Saints Day. This church holiday, on November 1, honors all Christian saints. The next day, November 2, is All Souls Day when prayers are offered for all the dead whose souls are in a special waiting place called Purgatory. Medieval Halloween festivities combine beautifully the customs of pagan Samhain with the Christian Hallows. Children wearing masks go *souling* from door to door, singing and begging for soul cakes for

Torches and candles lighting the way, nobles walk in an evening procession.

wandering spirits. If no treats are offered, beggars or souls play pranks. Halloween, then, reviews pleasures past. Nevertheless, it has a few surprises, such as colorful King Crispin presiding at the high table.

Jack-o'-Lanterns and a Bonfire in the Hall   Lights are the most important decoration in the Halloween Hall. Flames are thought to welcome good spirits and prevent evil ones from coming near, so every table has a Jack-o'-Lantern. Like the love lanterns of February, a turnip or squash is hollowed out, its sides carved into the shapes of eyes, nose, and mouth, so that a thick candle set within and lighted will shine through. Many lantern mouths are shaped as gracious grins. Some are forbidding scowls. (Pumpkin Jack-o'-Lanterns were not known in medieval Europe until well after the discovery of America. But they serve well for modern recreations of medieval Halloween.)

A large bright central light is placed near the high table. A candelabrum serves as an indoor bonfire, like in June's Midsummer Eve's festival fires.

King Crispin and the Revelers' Boot Baldrics   Ruling the high table is a guest disguised as King Crispin. Dressed magnificently in regal robes, crowned and flourishing a sceptor, he wears a heavy chain round his neck. Attached is a large medallion with the design of one big boot. King Crispin, really Saint Crispin, is the patron saint of Cordwainers—boot or shoemakers who work with Cordwain or Cordovan leather from Spain. Since St. Crispin's Day is a few days before Halloween, the two often are combined.

Guests come dressed in their own usual medieval costume. They do not wear masks. Only the seven people who will be the soulers have masks ready for later in the feast. Everyone pretends to be a member of King Crispin's court by wearing a purple baldric with a small gold boot or shoe painted or embroidered on it.

December's Hunt the Slipper and January's Play of St. George   With King Crispin's interest in shoes, it's not surprising that one Halloween game is Hunt the Slipper, also played in December at Christmas. (It is described on page 99.) After various feast foods are enjoyed, the Surveyor asks King Crispin whether mummers are welcome. Then the exuberant players, including a Hobby Horse, entertain the hall with a St. George Play, just as they do on Twelfth Night in January and on Midsummer Eve in June.

Souling and Soul Cakes   Soon after, the seven guest soulers put on their masks. Each carries a small basket to collect soul cakes. Walking briskly through the hall, the soulers chant:

Souling, souling, for soul cakes we go,
One for Peter, two for Paul,
Three for Him who made us all.
If you haven't got a cake, an apple will do,
If you haven't got an apple, give a pear or two.
If you haven't got a pear, then God bless you.

Soulers, still chanting, approach guests to collect gifts. Everyone gives a soul cake from a platter on the table. Soul cakes are flat, oval shortbread cookies with currants, cinnamon, and nutmeg. Or the guests offer fruits decorating the table. As soulers threaten amusing punishments to those who do not contribute, there is much hilarity in the souling. The seven baskets with their bounty are set in a circle around the bonfire candelabrum.

Divinations of February's Valentines and June's Midsummer   Halloween divinations are important during the feast and afterward, in the quiet of the night. Familiar Valentine's Day love divinations are also Halloween's: The Hemp Seed Throw, Yarrow, Night Yarrow, Eringoes, and Pillow Faces. At Summer's end, Midsummer Eve divinations are repeated: Diviner Eggs, Destiny Cakes, and the Midsummer Rose "He Loves Me," played with a late blooming, multi-petaled flower.

Nutcrack Night   One divination, however, is so popular that Halloween itself often is called Nutcrack Night. The nutcracking

Grain harvested with long-handled scythes is loaded onto a horse-drawn wagon in a field below a windmill.

is practiced two ways. For a small party in a house with a fireplace, a young man or woman ready to be married puts two whole walnuts or hazelnuts into the glowing embers. In a few minutes, the heated nuts will burst their shells. If one or both nuts crackle loudly, that is proof of hopeful love. If the nuts just burn, then the human love will briefly flame but soon perish. A rhyme recited while the couple watches the nuts is:

If he (or she) loves me, pop and fly;
If he (or she) hates me, lie and die.

At a large Halloween party, nut cracking is a table game. Using walnuts and nut crackers, each pair of guests crack nuts to foretell their future. If more half shells remain whole while allowing the nut meat to be removed, then the love will be perfect and true. If more shells shatter, so will the affection.

Apple Parings and Apple Bobbing Another love divination is apple paring. Using a whole apple and a small knife, each guest cuts a long spiral ribbon of apple skin, then throws it over his or her left shoulder. When it lands it will resemble the initial letter of the beloved's name.

Apple bobbing is a frolic, just as it is on July's St. Swithin's Day. On Halloween, divination is added. Each apple bobbed for is given the name of a desired mate. If the bobber succeeds in biting the apple on first try, then the love will thrive. If the apple is caught on the second bite, the love will exist only briefly. Success on the third chance means hate, not love. Four tries and more means no luck with that one; name another.

Crowdie Crowdie is a particularly delightful Halloween food. Six guests share a large bowl. A whipped sweet cream mixed with spiced apple sauce, crowdie has six objects dropped into it. Carefully cleaned beforehand in boiling water are two rings, two marbles, and two coins. Feasters use spoons to dip into the crowdie. Tasting so as to enjoy the crowdie but not swallow the "clue," the finder of a ring is soon to marry. The keeper of a coin will ever be wealthy. A marble means a cold single life. Spooning up nothing but crowdie foretells a life of sweet uncertainty.

Apple Candlelight Procession Halloween ends in the manner of August's Lammas festival. A candlelight procession three times round the hall precedes joyous farewells. At each circling, candle-carrying guests bow to King Crispin at the high table. The candleholders are shiny autumn apples. The candles must stay lighted for several minutes after the feast to scare evil spirits and cheer good souls.

CHAPTER XII

November: Catherning, or St. Catherine's Day

As guests file slowly to their seats in the darkened banquet hall, a fire juggler begins to twirl his lighted torches. One in each hand, he makes a circle with each. Now wheels of fire are on either side of him. Soon one whirls above his head, another near his feet. These flaming wheels are called *Catherine Wheels*. A fanfare sounds. An acrobat wearing silver anklebands turns cartwheels around the hall. These are also Catherine Wheels.

As each table's candles are lit, the lights catch more wheels on the ceiling and walls. The chandelier is a wagon wheel with many candleholders on the rim, held horizontally above the feasters by three strong chains. That, too, is a Catherine Wheel. Even the windows are covered with designs that make them *Catherine Windows*. Every Catherning feaster wears a wheel-shaped pin or a fabric spiked-wheel decoration sewn on to his or her costume. Catherning honors one of the most famous women saints, the noble, intelligent, learned St. Catherine of Alexandria. The Wheel is the symbol of her death in the fourth century.

Some people delight in Catherning because of their professions. She is the patron saint of lawyers, wheelwrights, rope makers, and carpenters. Most of all, she is revered as women's guide and guardian. She is patron saint of lace makers, spinners, unmarried women, and women students. Many Catherning, therefore, are women's feasts.

Lamb's Wool and the Cathern Bowl   One Catherning drink is Lamb's Wool. A large decorated bowl placed at the high table has a wheel suspended above it, held aloft by a wire frame. From the wheel at least twelve small apples on strings hover over the cider with its spices and frothy apples within. This is the *Cathern Bowl*. Even though Lamb's Wool fills the tankards at each table, everyone must have one small drink scooped from the Cathern Bowl before the end of the revels. This symbolic Cathern cup pledges a year of study, learning, and using elegant language. This unusual promise is a reminder that St. Catherine is said to have alone brilliantly argued against fifty of the most important scholars of the world and won.

Cathern Cakes and Wiggs   Wheel-shaped *Cathern Cakes* are rich with sugar, eggs, and caraway seeds. Sometimes they are triangular, representing the spikes on the wheel of her martyrdom. *Wiggs* are another wedge-shaped, delicious biscuit with currants, glazed orange, and caraway.

Feasters elegantly finger fish cut with notched knives and drink from cups called *mazers* while dogs beg at their feet.

Circles, Candle Jumps, and Fireworks All angles are rounded on St. Catherine's Day. Musicians sit not in a row but in a semicircle. Dancers form no straight lines but only circles. Servitors must not parade food in usual procession but must walk following a circular or serpentine pattern. This requires careful, amusing choreography.

A traditional Catherning game to musical accompaniment is the *Cathern Candle Jump*. A *Cathern Candle* is a wide candle securely set in a sturdy base. Placed in the middle of the floor, every guest must take a turn jumping over it. Everyone must be careful not to trip nor to tip it over nor to blow it out. The run to it and from it must be in a curved line. Successful jumpers have good fortune for the year.

A Catherning finale is fireworks. Weather permitting, guests bundle into their coats and watch the wheel-shaped firecrackers whirl. Naturally, these are called Catherine's Wheels. If cold or rain requires indoor farewells, then lights are extinguished one by one in the hall. The fire juggler ignites his torches. Slowly, then increasing in pace, the juggler twirls the circles of fire. Catherning begins and ends with radiance.

CHAPTER XIII

December: Christmas

MEDIEVAL Christmas is at least twelve times more splendid than any other holiday. One reason is that it lasts twelve full days. It begins on Christmas Eve and ends on Twelfth Night. Or we could count the days from Christmas Day to Twelfth Day, or Epiphany. When the evil king of Labora banished Christmas, he hurt his people twelve times over by transforming twelve days of celebration to a dozen days of hard work. But length of time is only one small part of the overall excellence of the Christmas season, which truly is the *Time of the Twelves.*

Whether to honor Christmas' twelve days or the twelfth month or the twelve apostles, each proper Christmas feast must have at least twelve holiday foods. There are twelve wassailings for the good health of trees and people. Twelve times a guest must pass beneath the *mistletoe* or under the *kissing bush.* Each guest gives and gets twelve gifts. Tables are set for twelves. Decorative holly branches are bunched in twelves. Twelve candelabras light the hall, or twelve groups of twelve candles shine brilliantly in this season, which is also the *Time of the Bee.*

That active insect is busy at least twelve hours of each day and all twelve months. Bees labor to create two magnificences: sweetness and light. From the nectar of flowers, bees produce honey. Beeswax candles light the darkness. Christmas customs resemble the bees' sweetness and light. Sweet foods are favorites: plum

"A hive for every house," a common medieval saying, testifies to the importance of bees' honey and wax.

pudding, *frumenty*, gingerbread *Yule dolls*, and hot elderberry wine. Light marks important rituals, such as in kindling the *Yule log* and igniting the elegant *Yule candle.*

In fact, medieval churchmen, like Saint Ambrose, compare the bees' habits and people's actions. The church is the hive of life in which faithful Christians labor ceaselessly for goodness. Christ's teachings are the "sweetness" of honey, and Christianity is the "light" of understanding.

Modern Christmas in the medieval manner still can be the Time of the Bee. But the medieval Christmas Time of the Twelves usually must be compressed into a modern single day's adventure.

Evergreenery in the Hall   In the banquet hall, greenery is everywhere. Evergreen branches decorate walls, windows, tables, and even the ceiling. Branches and sprigs of holly or laurel or yew are grouped in twelves. Sometimes one dozen small branches are held by a ribbon, or gaily colored bows or beads separate twelve leaves on a branch. Holly is the most important greenery. Like other evergreens, it keeps its leaves throughout the winter and appears never to change or to die.

Holly, sometimes called the holy bush, was important in winter celebrations even before the first Christmas. The Romans used holly decorations in their Saturnalia festivals.

While medieval Christmas feast halls have forest colors everyplace, there is no Christmas tree. Evergreen trees and Christmas are a modern combination. They did not become fashionable in England until the nineteenth century. Rather than a tree on the floor, a medieval *Christmas bush* is hung from the ceiling.

Mistletoe and the Kissing Bush   A bunch of green mistletoe hangs from a wire or slender chain either in the center of the room or from the top of a wide doorway. Often, mistletoe is the central greenery of the ceiling's *kissing bush*. This decoration is made with evergreen boughs arranged around a wooden frame, either square or round. Ribbons, small oranges and apples, nuts, and tiny sculptures cut from paper or stiff cloth hang among the branches.

Everyone who passes beneath it must kiss the person closest at the moment. Before the feast is over, each guest must have had at least twelve kisses.

Therefore, all guests entering the hall at Christmas and parading under the *kissing bush* begin the festivities with a kiss of friendship. Christmas is, after all, a celebration of love. Later in the feast, friends will exchange one of their twelve gifts beneath the kissing bush. This is a reminder of God's gift of Christ, and of the presents the Three Kings and the Three Shepherds brought to the Infant at Bethlehem.

While guests get their first Christmas kiss by walking under greenery, they must be careful not to walk over a green line, about ten feet in length, marked on the floor near the high table. This line made with green chalk, tape, or carefully laid carpet is called the *Christmas threshhold*. No one may cross it until it is first leaped over by a man with the whimsical name of *First Foot* or *Lucky Bird*.

Three couples dance exuberantly while musicians play recorder and drum.

First Foot, Lucky Bird, and Letting-In the Season Before the ceremonies of the feast begin, the Surveyor shouts "Wassail!" to all the guests, who then sit silently. The Surveyor loudly asks the most honored guest at the high table whether the feast may begin. The answer is "No! Not until First Foot crosses the Christmas threshhold!"

Suddenly, from the rear of the hall, a dark-haired man enters dressed in green. He is carrying an evergreen bough and wearing small bells on bands around each ankle. He is Lucky Bird or First Foot. Half dancing, half skipping, his ankle bells triumphantly ringing, he moves toward the high table. With a flourish, he jumps across the green line. He bows to the high table guests, removes his cap, and collects a coin from each. Then, with amusing antics, he passes from table to table so that each guest may place in his cap money for luck.

This is the *letting-in Christmas* ceremony. The green line on the floor stands for the threshhold or the floor beneath the door of a house. Outside is Christmas joy, which must be invited inside. Once the spirit of the season enters, all people within will have both pleasure and good luck for the coming year.

So the first man whose foot crosses the Christmas threshhold, which allows good fortune to fly in after him, is called Lucky Bird or First Foot. Usually he is a mummer; according to tradition, he must have brown or black hair, never red. (For Judas, the man who betrayed Christ, was thought to have been a redhead.) Feast after feast, Lucky Bird earns his pay as he merrily dances, tumbles, and crosses the Christmas threshhold.

The Yule Candle Next, a musical fanfare signals the Surveyor's start of feast ceremonials: wassail, salt, upper crust, credence, and hand washing. However, before Christmas food is served, a ceremonial light must be lit.

A gigantic candle is placed on the high table so that all in the hall can see and admire it. Usually it is specially and slowly crafted throughout the year from multiple colors of wax, taking twelve months to make, from Christmas time to Christmas. Usually it has in it some fragment of wax from last year's Yule candle. Or, twelve tall, slender taper candles can be bound together by fireproof cord and firmly set in a large shallow bowl. The Yule candle base is surrounded by holly. That is arranged, of course, in leaves or sprigs by twelves. And twelve ornaments made of thin metal in jaunty designs are pinned onto the candle. Slender sculptured triangles, stars, clowns' faces, lutes, boots, bears, wheels, and horseshoes are typical yule candle decorations.

The Surveyor lights this Christmas fire to the cheering shouts of "wassail! wassail!" Christmas light must be followed by Christmas sweetness. However, if the hall has a hearth, or fireplace, then another Christmas fire can be kindled: the Yule log.

The Yule Log The largest possible log the hearth will hold is brought into the hall on Christmas Eve and carefully lit. If properly tended, some part of that wood should be kept burning all twelve days of Christmas. Its last embers should still smolder on Twelfth Night. However, one small section of the log must be set aside and preserved as the first ignited kindling of next year's Yule log. This passing of the Yule light from year to year reminds Christmas revelers that the spirit of the season endures twelve months. It is simply rekindled during Christmas.

Frumenty and Posset, Yule Dolls and Perry A fanfare announces frumenty. This sweet simple dish is made of wheat, boiled milk, eggs, honey, and spices. With frumenty, one drinks *posset*, or rather, spoons it. Posset is so sumptuous a rich drink—made of milk, ale, egg, and nutmeg—that spooning it is neater and tastier than drinking it.

Next come the Yule dolls. These are gingerbread figures made with honey, nutmeg, saffron, lemon, and currants. The dolls' "arms" touch at the chest or stomach. Eyes and nose are raisins, the smiling mouth is a curl of orange peel. This is best eaten along with a tankard of pear juice or a light, sweet pear wine called *perry.*

Plum puddings, mince pies, and hot elderberry wine are among the other sweet Christmas courses, along with winter season meats, fish, and fowl. Peacock is roasted and refeathered to look alive. The claws and beak are painted glistening gold.

The Boar's Head Procession A single bell rings out to call the company to silence. Servitors march in a grand procession. They follow two servitors carrying a huge tray decorated with greenery; in the center is a boar's head. While the rest of the wild pig is eaten as pork or bacon, the head is roasted separately and presented with an apple or orange or lemon in its mouth. In elegant procession to the high table, passing each guest table in turn, the marchers sing the boar's head carol. It has a Latin refrain—*Caput apri defero, reddens laudes domino. Qui estis in convivio*—:

> The boar's head in hand bring I
> With garlands gay and rosemary,
> I pray you all sing merrily.

Wassailing with the Milly At the beginning of the feast, the Surveyor sings the first of three wassailings on Christmas. The second is called *Wassailing with the Milly*. A group of people circle the hall singing wassail songs and carols. They carry a large open box called the *Milly Box*. In its center is a small statue of the Virgin and Child. As the singers pass from table to table, every guest must give a "gift" to the "Milly," which means "my Lady," or "my Lady the Virgin." The present may be a coin, or small piece of fruit, or a more valuable gift such as a precious jewel. Later, these will be distributed to the needy. Giving to the Milly assures good luck.

The wassailers then sing wish songs:

> We wish you a joyous Christmas
> Very happy New Year!
> Pouches full of money,
> Barrels full of beer,
> Stout cows and pigs
> To cheer you all year!

Similar wishes for health and abundance are the message of the third wassailing. This is directed not toward people but to trees. Surrounding a tree branch held high by one of the singers, the wassailers cheer it and command it to be fruitful:

> Stand mute at root!
> Bear high to the sky.
> Every twig, hold apples big.
> Every bough, bear fruit enow!

In the snowy inn yard, a man and woman slaughter a pig for pork and bacon; guests watch from the windows.

Christmas Customs and the Winter World The three Christmas wassailings happily combine Christmas ritual with earlier pagan rituals for fertility of trees and animals. In some countries, saluting animals at Christmas is so important that no one may eat at a Christmas feast until the animals are first fed. Sometimes the first portion cut from the plum pudding or frumenty or Yule doll must be given to a favorite farm cow or horse or pig. Then the animals must be provided with extra portions of their regular food to commemorate the holiday. Christmas bird feeders set in trees near the house allow birds extra food in the cold of winter, and people pleasure observing the birds' bounty.

Cherishing animals is the ancient requirement to give gifts to beasts (and also to trees) in winter so they will be vigorous and productive in spring. Paired with this pagan idea is Christian thanks to animals, the infant Jesus' "first friends" in time of need at the first Christmas.

Bee in the Middle: A Christmas Game   Between courses, games entertain both players and watchers. Some of the oldest Christmas games that seem to be mere joyous entertainments are actually remakings of early religious rituals. An apparently simple game played by both adults and children is *Bee in the Middle*.

At least twelve players sit on the floor in a circle. Each player sits fairly close to the next. Another player, the Bee, sits in the middle of the circle, wearing a mask with long antennae, or feelers, rising into the air above it. These are made of twisted wires bent back upon themselves so there are no sharp edges, or they are crafted of stiff cardboard. The Bee sits with legs folded in front or under, and must remain seated this way while playing. One at a time, everyone in the circle tries to touch the bee and not get "stung." The bee does not know from which direction a touch will come. The bee therefore tries to "sting" by touching with its feelers or catching the toucher by hand. The Bee may rock back and forth in any direction but never uncross legs or stand up. Each player tries to avoid being caught by surprising the Bee with a touch or gentle hit. The player the Bee "stings" by antenna or catches by hand is the next Bee in the Middle. And so the game goes on.

Meanings of Christmas Games and Blind Man's Buff   The bee, of course, is the insect which gives sweetness and light. In this game, the bee is an animal captured in a circle, the object of much teasing and taunting. This ritual game has been played for so many hundreds of years that it is thought old and traditional even in the Middle Ages. Other animals "in the middle"—such as *Bull in the Middle*—remind us that originally this game was part of a pagan animal sacrifice. An ancient Roman god could take an animal form. And the sacrifice of certain animals sacred to the gods might allow goodness and strength to endure on earth. Christian folklore reinterprets such ideas especially at Christmas, when, according to tradition, God takes on the form of a human child. Later the sweetness of his learning and the light of his law lead to his captivity and sacrifice.

Few people playing *Bee in the Middle* know how it came to be a Christmas game. Those who know it as *Frog in the Middle* will be surprised this game is so very old.

A similar, seemingly simple Christmas game is *Blind Man's Buff*. Twelve or more players form a large circle, each facing the center. One player stands inside the circle and is masked so that he or she can see nothing. The mask often imitates an animal's face, such as a deer or wolf. The masked Blind Man, or Blind Woman, is turned around several times and then must "catch" a player in the circle and correctly name him or her. In the mean-while, players try to touch or lightly hit or "buffet" the Blind Man. Then they run back to their places in the circle. The person the Blind Man catches and identifies becomes the next masked Blind Man.

Hunt the Slipper A third Christmas circle game called *Hunt the Slipper* requires that the guests be seated in a tight ring. They may sit on the floor with legs stretched out in front of them, or they may use chairs set in a circle. One guest is called *Slipper Soul*, and stands within the circle with a shoe or slipper in hand. Every-one in the circle pretends to be a shoemaker or cobbler, busily sewing leather. Slipper Soul chants:

Cobbler, cobbler,
Mend my shoe!
Make it all anew.
Three stitches will do!

The shoe then is handed to one "cobbler." Slipper Soul must close his eyes tightly for a few seconds. The cobblers pass the shoe from one to another, trying to hide it from Slipper Soul's view. If they are seated on the floor, they pass it beneath their knees. If they are on chairs, they pass it behind their backs. Those who are not holding the shoe pretend that they are. When Slipper Soul opens his eyes he must guess who has the shoe. Since everyone seems to be passing it, the choice is hard. When Slipper Soul correctly identifies the cobbler who has the three-stitch-mended shoe, that player becomes the next Slipper Soul.

Democratic Customs Variations of these Christmas circle games as Hunt the Slipper, Blind Man's Buff, and Bee in the Middle are played with enthusiasm in noble courts as well as in country cottages. The "shoe" may be an elegant silk slipper embroidered with pearls and emeralds, or a plain leather work-boot. The game is the same. One marvel of medieval celebrations is the stability of their structure. Details differ from social class to class and from castle to manor house to country cottage. But traditional customs are constant. Real young shoemakers play "cobblers" in *Hunt the Slipper* and so do noble young knights and ladies.

At Christmas this equality of celebration has special importance. It reminds every reveler that the greatest of kings may be hidden in the humblest home. Wealth does not create worthiness. The simplest goodness is as significant as the grandest piety.

Humble Pie Trumpet fanfares introduce a special Christmas dish called *humble pie*. All Christmas feasters, rich or poor, can afford to bake this meat pie. Medieval humble pie has nothing to do with being humble. Today, however, "to eat humble pie" means to give in and submit to a higher authority, or to withdraw to a humbler position. But medieval "humble" or "umble" simply means the innards of an animal, known today as tripe. These innards are favorite delicacies for noble medieval hunters as well as for poor farmers. Cooked for many hours, Christmas umbles are then baked in a pie. The sweet crust is pierced with holes in cross shapes. Umble, of course, sounds like humble, and this traditional delight has fed pauper as well as king. Therefore it is understandable that people have thought humble pie to be the food only of the lowly and the poor.

The Play of the Three Shepherds A loud bell rings. The Surveyor announces, "All lights in the hall are to be snuffed out!" Everyone is silent. One by one, the Surveyor lights twelve small candles. The darkened hall is just light enough for every guest to see the silvery fluttering wings of an angel. This angel is a banquet guest or actor announcing the short *Play of the Three Shepherds*. Poor shepherds as well as rich kings were the first to learn of Christmas. Three star-led kings from the East came carrying gifts to the child in the manger; a play commemorating this is presented on Twelfth Night. Three angel-led shepherds also viewed the marvelous babe. This is celebrated with a play on Christmas Day, such as this fourteenth-century playlet from Rouen, France.

The Christmas angel, who carries a candle, is dressed in flowing white robes with wide, silver-painted wings. The angel speaks from "above," standing on a tall table which is invisible in the darkened hall, or calls loudly from a balcony:

Fear not! I bring you tidings of great joy.
This day in the City of David, a savior is born.
You'll find the child wrapped in swaddling clothes,
And lying in a manger.

Now twelve more angels sing joyously:

Glory to God in the Highest	*Gloria in excelsis deo*
And peace on earth	*Et in terra pax*
And good will to men.	*Hominibus bone voluntatis.*

An angel announces to a simple shepherd that Christ
is born; the dog also listens.

The Three Shepherds, also carrying candles, say "Let us go and
see what has been promised. Let us draw close to the manger."
They move near to a small curtained manger. They are stopped
by two midwives who ask, "Whom do you seek in the manger,
oh shepherds. Tell us!" (In the original Latin, the question reads:
quem quaeritis in prosepe, pastores. Dicite.)

The shepherds reply, "The savior, the infant Lord, as the Angel
told us." As the midwives draw back the curtain, the shepherds
gasp in wonderment. The midwives then say, "Here is the little one
the prophet Isaiah spoke of long ago. Go now, and announce that
he is born." The shepherds bow, worship the mother and child
in the manger, and cry triumphantly, "Alleluia! Alleluia! Now
we know the truth of the prophecy. Alleluia!"

As the shepherds leave to tell the good news, bells ring wildly. Hand bells or church bells ring in twelve strokes followed by another twelve. Then three rings and another three. If there are no large bells, small jingling bells are shaken rhythmically. These bells are often called the *Virgin's Welcome.* And sometimes they are called the *Devil's Death Knell.*

Christmas bells ringing the news of the birth of the Holy Child bring Christmas revelries to their end. Really, of course, it is their beginning. For Christmas is the twelfth month, twelve-day cele-bration of Twelve. It ends in January on Twelfth Night. Celebrat-ing medieval holidays allows us to imitate the glorious circle of the seasons. The sweetness and light of the Christmas Time of the Bee does not end until the following month. And with the new year, the cycle begins again, as in the first chapter of this book, at Twelfth Night.

CHAPTER XIV

Transformations and Illusions

THINKING about medieval holidays and festivals is splendid. But the best delights are yet to come when you translate the medieval idea into the modern reality. Recreating a medieval holiday's fabulous feast is not difficult or expensive. But it requires ingenuity. There are three major adventures. One is decorating the hall. Second is costuming the people. Third is preparing the medieval food. All three become delights if you are willing to practice medieval *rotation*.

Rotation   Picture a wheel with spokes and a hub, standing in the air. Imagine a chair on top of the wheel. Call that seat a throne, and sit a princess on it, wearing a golden crown. Picture the bottom of the wheel. See two hands clutching the rim, holding on tight. Attached to the hands are the arms, body, and hopeful face of a young man, dangling in air. Slowly and carefully turn your wheel. What was up now is down. What was below is above. Off flies the royal gold crown. If the princess does not grab the wheel rim, she too will be spilled into the air along with her noble throne. Up scrambles the one who patiently held on at the bottom.

This is the medieval *Wheel of Fortune.* The one who rotates it is *Lady Fortune.* Moving her wheel at times we cannot predict, and in ways we do not understand, her spinning plan is mysterious.

Therefore those who have good fortune living at the top of the wheel of life may suddenly fall. Those down below may ascend to grandeur. Fortune's Wheel is the medieval reminder that nothing lasts forever, and nothing is impossible. Anything unfortunate now soon may be perfect. For example, in recreating medieval holidays it is fortunate to have the right architecture, a church, temple, school, or home magnificently Gothic, Romanesque, or Byzantine. Arches, vaults, and stained glass windows are ready background for medieval celebration. However many holiday re-creators have uninteresting modern rooms with inappropriate small tables and ugly fluorescent lights. They have a wonderful chance to practice rotation. "How lucky we do not have the restrictions of the ready-made setting. We have the opportunity to transform the dull to the magnificent. Banners, candles, costumes, and our own cleverness will make our pleasure in the event all the greater."

Rotation requires imagining excellence on the other side of apparent trouble. For instance, you may need a long, narrow table for the high table in your feast hall. You cannot buy one. However, there is a tall door leading down to the cellar stairs. Imagine it rotated, on its side. It resembles a long, narrow table. Remove it from its hinges, and rotate it horizontally. Place the door on two small tables of equal height, and well-spaced to balance the door-table. Remove the knob; or simply disguise it with greenery as a table decoration. By rotation, you have created a banquet high table.

Diamond crowns and jeweled tiaras can be crafted similarly. Suppose no glittering head pieces are buyable or borrowable, but your friend has a costume jewelry necklace. Another has a wide, stiff, fancy, jeweled bracelet. Rotate either the necklace or the bracelet, literally turning it upside down as you raise it to your head. Anchor your new crown to your hair with bobbypins, or attach it to a skull cap with thin wires so it stands upright, while hatpins hold the cap to your hair.

Decorating the Hall with Banners and Wall Hangings
Bright banners vivify even the barest walls. Obtain large pieces of solid color felt. Five feet high by four feet wide is a useful size for each banner. Whatever amount you need, obtain nearly double the quantity so that the decorations for the banners can be cut from the same felt. For a large hall you might wish to have twelve banners. Banner backgrounds certainly can be all the same color with different colored designs and decorations on each. Or you might select four main colors, with three banners made in each color, such as red, gold, green, and purple.

1. Cut the 5' x 4' banner background, allowing an extra 4 to 6 inches for a hem at the banner top. This will allow a wooden dowel or light metal rod to be inserted through it to make the banner easier to hang. Sew the hem or staple the banner to its wooden strut.

2. Create *heraldic* designs. On a sheet of newspaper, draw a large shield. This will be your pattern for most of the decorations. From the leftover felt, cut twelve shields, according to your paper pattern, making sure that you will have brightly contrasting designs on each banner background: a gold shield on a purple banner, or red on green.

3. Divide six shields in half from top to bottom with a line of contrasting colored felt. Separate the other six shields into quarters with a "cross" of colored felt.

4. From the leftover felt scraps, make designs to fill the half shields and quarter shields. On sheets of paper, design, for example, a unicorn or a lion standing on its hind legs. Then trace these onto the felt. Place a gold lion on a purple half shield, or a red unicorn on a green quartering. Design small geometric shapes or simple flowers, such as a rose, lily, or thistle. Or draw farm implements, such as a sickle, or plow, or harrow. Or you could make chain links, crosses, stars, bells, chimneys, helmets, trees, or apples, or perhaps find a sign important to you—a basket or a bear.

5. Paste or sew the designs on the shields. Then glue or sew the shields to the banners.

Naturally, you are free to put two shields on a single banner. Or one large gold lion on a purple background. Or a lion and unicorn holding a shield between them. Be ingenious! Here are a few more design inspirations:

Elaborate wall hangings sometimes are obtainable ready-made in bedding and housewares stores. Bedspreads with strong geometric designs in the medieval or Renaissance manner are particularly useful. With fringes and pompons they are available for rotation from bed to wall. Pushpins affix them. Or, sew a hem at the top for slipping through a long curtain rod or wooden dowel for easy hanging. Add heraldic designs cut from cardboard or paper.

Lighting the Hall   Candles are ideal for recreating the proper medieval atmosphere. Large, dripless candles in sturdy holders can be grouped together in important places. In arranging them, consider safety and dramatic visibility.

In addition to wax candles, oil lamps are effective soft lights. In a metal, glass, or ceramic bowl, a wick either floats on or is suspended in vegetable or mineral oil.

If candles and oil lamps do not give enough light for a particular game or festivity—or if fire prevention laws prohibit open flames—then see whether your room has a "dimmer" switch or rheostat for electric lights. If so, set it on "low." Use flame-shaped bulbs to dignify ordinary electric lamps or chandeliers.

Arranging the Tables   All shapes and types of tables are proper for medieval feasting. Round tables, square, oval, and rectangular appear in medieval illustrations. The most common shape, however, is the long, slender, rectangular *banquet board,* or *refectory table.* This is a useful shape for the high table, for the most honored celebrants, and also for the regular guest tables, which are called the *sideboards.* Long "cafeteria" tables or "picnic" tables can be disguised with cloths to look medieval. But ingenuity and effort will create a long refectory table for the banqueting. Again, rotate a tall, old door to table height and set it on two smaller tables to support it. Or place the door on carpenters' saw horses; such temporary medieval tables were called *horse and saddle tables.*

For the sake of the entertainments and ease of serving, an ideal arrangement of all tables is a "U." The cross bar of the "U" is the high table. The legs of the U are the guests' tables, the sideboards. Depending on the available space, guests may be seated on chairs or benches only on one side of the table. All face the inside of the U where the performers will play their parts.

However, round tables placed in a large oval design may be equally effective. Three necessities determine table placement. 1) Make the high table the center of the ceremonies. Here the Surveyor will stand, directing the festivities. 2) Be sure every guest can see the ceremonial food service, and all entertainment. 3) Let the arrangement seem gracious and artful.

Decorations on the Table   Simple white tablecloths are adequate. Bed sheets, particularly in rich colors as maroon, burgundy, or forest green, also make interesting table covers. For the high table, use a geometrically patterned cloth such as a damask, or a tapestry made with a washable bedspread in a proper medieval or Renaissance pattern. An oriental carpet runner is a dramatic table covering over a white or colored cloth. The rug, of course, requires special cleaning before and after use.

There need be no platters except bread trenchers, cut round or oval or square. There need be no cutlery at all. For drinking ciders and wines, medieval-style metal tankards or mugs can be bought.

Equally effective, correct drinking vessels are crystal-cut glasses or tall-stemmed water glasses.

Each table ought to have a few small spice dishes. One contains dried sweet basil, another cinnamon sugar, and a third ground mustard or salt. Greenery, fresh fruit, small chunks of cheese, and shelled nuts make good decorations as well as useful nibbles. These may be arranged on metal platters, or directly on the cloth in an artistic design.

Since all foods will be eaten with fingers, a large fabric napkin must be provided for each guest.

Ceremonial Objects on the High Table: The Salt and the Aquamanile The salt must be an extraordinary object. Fine modern salts can be rotated from unpromising sources. An elaborate model ship from a child's toy collection makes a ship-shaped salt called a *nef*. Painted gold, it will look more important than its humble origins. An ornate flower vase or large, excessively decorated, covered candy dish also might do. A good place to find a salt is a second-hand or antique shop, or a basement or attic where old, useless gifts are stored. An object large enough to command attention, yet too fancy or too decorative for normal use often makes a good salt. After all, it is not merely the salt holder but the marker of magnificence: the most important people sit above the salt, all others sit below the salt. Necessity may transform an old absurdity into a ceremonial extravaganza.

For the hand-washing ceremony, the aquamanile can be a simple water pitcher. Use a large one, one-third filled with warm water in which you float sweet, crushed herbs or flowers. A large shallow bowl must be carried with it to catch the water poured over the guests' fingers. A long linen towel ought to be available nearby. Two dish towels or tea towels sewn together end on end work well. An even better aquamanile is an amusing animal-shaped pitcher. A lion or dragon or bear aquamanile may not be easy to find but usually can be rotated from out of the kitchen, where it may be a cookie jar, or from a flower shop, where it may start as a plant holder.

Costumes and Rotation Robes Some people who recreate medieval holidays have easy access to theatrical costumes. They simply get fitted with beautiful medieval and Renaissance silks, velvets, brocades, and jewels. They are ready to act their medieval parts in the theater of the feast. Thanks to their local Shakespearean acting or opera group, or professional costume rental company, they expend no ingenuity in creating their medieval garb.

Other people have three choices. One is to perform medieval festivities in modern clothes. This is a pity. To truly appreciate the glories of medieval celebration, every sense must be satisfied. Modern clothes cannot match the delight in the sense of sight or the sense of touch as well as the simplest attempt at medieval costumery.

A second choice for the costume-needy is a form of robe rotation. Take something which exists, and turn it to a new purpose. A choir robe is an excellent beginning. So is a velour or velvet bathrobe for a man or a woman. Several items added to a simple robe transform it into a medieval gown suitable for a prince or princess.

1. *Collars*: Fur collars from old coats and sweaters can be sewn on or attached with safety pins. Other fine neck decorations are made from colored beads, gold and silver chains, jewelry ropes, jeweled necklaces and medallions. Either sew these on, or wear them loosely, cascading down the chest.
2. *Sleeve Cuffs*: Sew or pin a wide piece of imitation fur, cut from an old coat hem, or bought by the yard at a fabric store. Or sew or pin a wide piece of silver or gold braid on the outside of the cuff, or sew it on the cuff lining. Such borders may be salvaged from old drapes, or bought from a local dime store.
3. *Hems*: Sew or pin on an imitation fur border.
4. *Belts*: Old fashioned drape tie-backs with tassels are excellent. So are chain links, available by the yard from hardware stores,

Showing three generations of court costumes with furs, enormous sleeves, heavy neck chains, and jeweled hats, a king greets his daughter and grandchildren.

as well as metal dog leashes. Jeweled necklaces, two or three attached together, or strings of pearls, can be worn loosely around the waist, or draped gracefully, lower toward the hips.

5. *Shoes*: Wear ballet slippers, low-heeled boots, or sandals. Underneath, tights are more useful than socks.

6. *Hats*: Obtain a skull cap or a beret. Add a bright costume jewel to it, which should rest above the forehead. Or add a long feather, which should curve down the side of the head toward the neck. Or trim the cap with a border of mock fur. If you wish a regal crown or tiara, rotate one.

7. *Other Gorgeous Additions*: Remember that both medieval men and women wear laces, jewelry, soft and elegant fabrics, embroideries, and furs.

Costume Patterns, Fabrics, and Miparti   A rotation robe is fine for medieval celebrations. Even more splendid is the third costume choice, also a form of rotation. Make your own, because necessity creates the opportunity.

Consider this basic pattern—a tunic with wide, flared sleeves.

You have a choice of length, depending upon what social class you intend to represent, and what fashion from which country in which year you intend to duplicate. Naturally, histories of costumery will distinguish among twelfth-century German costumes, thirteenth-century Parisian, fourteenth-century Burgundian, and fifteenth-century Florentine. However, a general "medieval" costume is this basic tunic, which may be decorated in various wonderful ways. Generally, women wear long gowns, men wear short. Before adding decorations of collars, cuffs, hems, and belts, which are similar to those for rotation gowns, you must make two important decisions.

Fabric is first. Any inexpensive, brightly colored cloth will do. Wool, cotton, muslin, felt, and burlap are all fine, depending on the season in which you're wearing the costume, and upon your budget. Unexpected sources for sumptuous fabrics are upholstery and curtain shops. Exquisite fabrics in remnants too small to cover a sofa but perfect for a person are available inexpensively.

The second costume decision after fabric and color is *miparti*. Miparti is the noteworthy fashion in which half the body is clothed in one color, and the other half in another color. Imagine the basic tunic with a line drawn right through the middle, down from the neckline to the hem. The right side is an elaborate red brocade, the left side is gold. The hem on the left, however, is red, and on the right, it is gold.

For making many costumes at once, miparti allows great variations speedily and cheaply. For twelve costumes, for example, select six separate fabrics. After cutting the basic pattern for each of the twelve, divide each tunic in half, and recombine each half-tunic with a pleasing contrasting color.

Miparti fashion also affects the legs. Each is a different color. A simple solution is to obtain strong, opaque dancing tights. For each costume, use two sets of contrasting colors. Carefully cut the right leg from one, the left leg from the other. Wear the panty plus remaining leg of both. If the tights are well made, two pairs may serve two people. Each pair of tights is cut exactly in half, one leg plus half a pant securely sewn to the contrastingly colored other half.

Whether you select a single color basic tunic, or miparti, there are numerous variations that can transform the simple to the spectacular.

1. *Collars*: Variously shaped collars may be cut from imitation fur or felt. Use any simple or fancy fabric.
   a. Collars may be *coronal*, like a simple crown around the neck, standing away from the tunic.

   b. Or they may be *chevral*, resembling a chevron or V shape.

   c. Or make them *dagged*. *Dagging* is a design resembling an upside down castle wall (officially, that is called *crenellation*) or teeth spaced with every other one missing.

   d. Or the collar may be *scintillated*, like rays of the sun.

   e. Or *scalloped*, like sea shells set side by side.

2. *Sleeves*: Make interesting sleeve decorations with cuff borders at the edge of the sleeve near the wrist. As for rotation robes:
   a. Sew on a wide band of mock fur, or braiding, or embroidered ribbon.
   b. A variation is to sew the band *inside* the sleeve edge, so this lining will show when the hands are raised.
   c. Attach to the outer cuff a band of chevrons, dagging, scintillations, or scallops, cut from the same cloth as the sleeve. Or use a different fabric.
   d. Try sleeve piercing. Cut a long slit from below the shoulder to near the cuff, and sew a border on the cut edges. Wear a bright shirt with full billowy sleeves beneath the tunic. The undersleeves will show through the piercing when the arms move. It works even more dramatically with two or three piercings on each sleeve.
3. *Hems*: Whether short tunic or long, the border is easily ornamented.
   a. Use imitation fur, wide gold braid, or jeweled borders.
   b. Cut a fabric in the shapes of chevrons, dags, scintillations, or scallops.
4. Men's and women's costumes may be belted at either the waist or the hips.
5. *Hats*: Hennin, chaperone, and *chaplet*. While certain gown and cape styles serve a medieval princess as well as prince, and townswoman as well as townsman, some hat styles are only for one sex. A fine basic, popular medieval hat for girls and women is the *hennin*. The *chaperone* with *lirapipe* is a good basic hat for boys and men. Both men and women may wear *chaplets*.

    a. The hennin: The hennin is a tall, fabric-covered cone that looks like a most elegant dunce cap. A delicate silk scarf or veil suspended from the hennin's peak hangs down the wearer's back. To make a hennin, shape a cardboard or oaktag cone to fit the head. Or buy a styrofoam cone such as florists use for flower arrangements, available in a variety store. Cover the cone with a fabric matching the costume. Attach the hennin to a cap, which then can be pinned securely to the hair. If the hennin is too heavy or too tall to sit securely, attach ribbon or elastic for tying beneath the chin. The pinnacle scarf may be the same color as the hennin, or a complementary hue.

    b. The chaperone: The chaperone is a graceful hat resembling a turban. To make a chaperone, begin with a *roundlet*, a fabric doughnut filled with cotton or scraps of paper, which fits on the head above the hairline. Twice wind a long piece of cloth around this roundlet and around the wearer's head. Secure the cloth to the roundlet with a fancy jewel pin. Allow a fabric "tail" to hang down the back, or to be draped over the shoulder. A very long chaperone tail is called a *lirapipe*.

    c. The chaplet: A cloth band is worn at the hairline or across the forehead and around the head. Jewels, sequins, and cut-out designs may adorn it. A wreath-of-flowers chaplet is perfect for spring and summer celebrations.

6. *Shoes, boots, and poulaines*:

    a. As with rotation robes, wear ballet slippers, boots, or sandals.

    b. Make *poulaines*. These are shoes with long, tapered toe points, reinforced by wires inside, so the points curl up so as to not trip the wearers. Start with ballet shoes. Use the same colored soft leather or suede, and fashion a slender cone or flattened triangle. Insert wire to the tip, and anchor it inside the triangle with both stitches and masking tape. Sew the triangle to the ballet shoe. Adjust the tip angle to avoid interfering with walking.

    c. Underneath the foot gear, wear tights, either plain or miparti.

Medieval rotation is helpful for decorating the hall and costuming the guests. Yet one more preparation is necessary before a medieval celebration begins: the glorious medieval foods and drinks.

CHAPTER XV

Medieval Recipes

MANY of the dishes in *Medieval Holidays and Festivals* can be created just from the descriptions in the text. Mayday's Jack-in-the-Green gingerbread cakes, for example, appear in various medieval recipes in forms startlingly similar to those in modern "gingerbread man" recipes. To recreate this medieval delicacy, simply decorate a modern gingerbread man cookie with a wreath of bright green icing or sprinkles.

Other medieval dishes, however, present opportunities for culinary adventures. The ingredients are not hard to find, and some of the contrasts in taste and spice are surprising. The recipes here allow for a fine variety of texture, aroma, and taste, and range from the very simple instructions for *fruyte fritours* to the more complex baking instructions for *rose-petal bread*.

Here are a few medieval kitchen hints for the modern cook.

Delight in Food Color   Remember that the chief cook was considered a food artist. In addition to natural colors of fruits, vegetables, creams, and meats, the cook would add natural "food paint" or color to invigorate paler or duller hues, or to create special illusions. Today's natural vegetable dyes are simply the modern versions of medieval food paints, which were created by boiling flowers or leaves in water or white wine. For medieval red food coloring, rose petals were used; for yellow and gold, saffron or dandelion; for green, mint, parsley, spinach, or hazel leaves; for blue, heliotrope or turnsole; for lavender, violets.

Plan for Artistic Contrasts No matter how simple or ambitious your menu is, try to assure that a sweet food follows a sharp and spicy dish; a heavier meat follows a lighter, fresh vegetable; a bright food follows one with blander color. Since the medieval feast was really dramatic and theatrical, try to serve a major spectacle dish, such as a refeathered roasted goose (or peacock or pheasant), ceremonially presented as the high point in the festivity.

Think About Food Ceremony Even a meager budget and restricted kitchen time can yield elegantly presented festival creations. A simple, inexpensive, easily prepared menu would contain much fresh fruit, nuts, and cheese, all set out in elaborate platter designs, the more whimsical the more splendid. From a professional baker, order one extravagant pastry or marzipan subtletie in a shape suitable to the month's celebration.

Present Elegant Tastings—Not Gargantuan Gorgings
Each of the following recipes will serve a small portion to at least twelve people.

Breads and Cakes
Payn Pur-Dew
Caraway Seed Shortbread
Rose-Petal Bread
Destiny Cakes
Circletes: Almond Cardamom
Cakes

Meat, Fish, and Fowl
Fruyte Buf: Fruit Beef
Sweet Capon
Dukess Wynges
Sweete Fysshe en Doucette

Rice and Pasta
Peppermint Rice
Pasta and Apricot Butter

Delectables
Swithin Cream
Jusselle Date
Almoundyn Eyroun

Fruits and Vegetables
Fruyte Fritours
Canel Cucumber
Chardwardon
May Sallat

Drinks
Mulled Apple or Pear Cider
Lamb's Wool

BREADS AND CAKES

Payn Pur-Dew

The name means either God's bread or lost bread; this is a medieval version of modern french toast.

7 fresh eggs, separated
4 tablespoons heavy cream
   or milk
¼ teaspoon salt
¼ teaspoon cinnamon
½ teaspoon ground cumin
12 slices whole wheat, rye,

or pumpernickle bread
cut into 4 squares or
4 triangles each
3 tablespoons brown sugar
¼ pound butter for sautéing
   in a heavy frying pan or
   skillet

1. Slowly heat the butter in the heavy frying pan or skillet, being careful not to let it burn.
2. With a fork or rotary beater, beat the egg yolks with the cream or milk. Add the egg whites. Beat again.
3. Stir in the salt, cinnamon, and cumin.
4. Dip the bread pieces in the spiced egg until they are completely coated and remove them with a spatula.
5. Sauté the bread on both sides in the melted butter until golden brown.
6. Remove them to a rack or the serving platter and sprinkle them with brown sugar. Serve warm.

Caraway Seed Shortbread

3 cups all-purpose un-
   bleached white or whole
   wheat flour
½ cup sugar
2 teaspoons cinnamon
½ teaspoon powdered
   cardamom
½ teaspoon powdered
   ginger

¾ teaspoon allspice
½ teaspoon salt
1¼ tablespoons caraway
   seeds
1 cup butter at room
   temperature

1. Preheat oven to 350°.
2. Combine sugar, cinnamon, cardamom, ginger, allspice, salt, and caraway seeds. Separate into two equal portions; set one aside.
3. On a strong, clean kneading surface, such as a kitchen counter or breadboard, mix by hand ½ of the spice mixture into the flour.
4. Squeeze the butter in your hands, and bit by bit, add the spiced flour, working it into the butter on the board. Take time to thoroughly integrate the spices into the butter mixture.
5. Press the batter into an 8″ square shallow baking pan.
6. With a sharp knife indent the surface of the batter to outline "fingers," about 2″ long by 1″ wide. Also make several shallow cuts crosswise on each finger.
7. Sprinkle the reserved spice mixture on the surface of the batter.
8. Bake 1 hour or less until firm and yellow, or very light brown.
9. Cool in the pan. Break the shortbread into fingers, and serve.
10. Often tasting better when several days old, caraway shortbread keeps beautifully when stored in an airtight container.

Rose-Petal Bread

2 packages active dry yeast
2 cups warm water
6 tablespoons honey
7 cups unbleached white or whole wheat flour
1⅔ tablespoons coarse salt
6 whole eggs plus 1 egg yolk
1 cup currants, softened in warm water
6 tablespoons melted butter or oil
butter for greasing bowls and cookie sheet

1½ teaspoons dried rosemary
1½ teaspoons dried basil
½ teaspoon cinnamon
⅔ or 1 cup finely chopped rose petals (between 1 and 2 doz. red roses)
See note, next page
several drops red food paint, prepared as the medieval baker would, in advance (see page 116)

1. Sprinkle the yeast on ½ cup of the warm water in a mixing bowl. Stir in the honey. Let it stand for 5 minutes.
2. Add the remaining warm water and about 2½ to 3 cups of flour. Beat by hand with a wooden spoon, about 200 strokes. Cover with a damp towel, put in a warm place, and let the dough rise 30 to 45 minutes, or until it is doubled in bulk.

3. Punch the dough down. Beat in the salt, melted butter, and 5 whole eggs plus 1 egg yolk. Stir in the currants.

4. In a mortar with a pestle, crush the rosemary, basil, cinnamon, and rose petals to make a paste. Add this herb mixture to the dough and knead it, blending well. (The bread should be a delicate rose hue. If the color from the rose petals isn't strong enough, use the red food color sparingly).

5. Beat in the remaining flour, using a spoon. Knead the dough until it comes away from the sides of the bowl.

6. Turn the dough out onto a lightly floured board or slab of marble and knead it until smooth, shiny, or elastic, about 10–12 minutes, adding small amounts of flour if the dough becomes too sticky to handle.

7. Place the dough in a buttered bowl. Cover with a damp towel. Let it rise in a warm place until doubled in bulk, about 50 minutes.

8. Punch the dough down. Cover it, and let it rise again until doubled in bulk, about 30 minutes.

9. Again, punch the dough down. Turn it out onto a floured surface and let it rest for 5 minutes. Shape the dough into 1 or 2 free-form, turbanlike curls or twists. Place on a buttered cookie sheet. Cover lightly with a towel and let it rise in a warm place until doubled in bulk, about 25 minutes.

10. Preheat the oven to 375°. Brush the loaf or loaves with the remaining whole egg, lightly beaten. Bake for about 50 minutes or until nicely browned and the loaf sounds hollow when rapped lightly on the top with knuckles. Transfer the rose-petal bread to a rack and allow it to cool.

NOTE: It is advisable to obtain roses, either from a florist or a garden, that have not been sprayed with pesticides.

Destiny Cakes

These elderberry funnel cakes are simple fried crullers, made with batter that is passed through a funnel or tube, making amusing, fantastic, or "divination" shapes.

3 eggs, well beaten	2 cups milk
½ teaspoon salt	4 cups flour

2 teaspoons, or slightly less, baking powder
½ cup elderberry preserves or plum jam
2 cups vegetable oil for "deep frying" in a fryer

A funnel or pastry tube with nozzle measuring ½″ in diameter
6 tablespoons honey

1. Add the salt to the beaten eggs. Stir the eggs briskly into the milk.
2. Stir the baking powder into the flour.
3. Mix most of the milk and the eggs with the flour.
4. Add the elderberry or plum preserves to the mixture. If the resulting batter is too thick to run easily through the funnel or pastry tube, add more of the milk and egg mixture. If the batter is too thin to hold its shape—the consistency ought to resemble a thick pancake batter—add a small extra amount of flour.
5. Into hot oil in a deep, wide, frying pan, pipe the fruit batter in imaginative shapes, making initials or designs. Fry until golden.
6. Remove from oil. Drain. Lightly drizzle with honey, and serve each cake warm.

Circletes—Almond Cardamom Cakes

1 cup butter
⅔ cup brown sugar
1 beaten egg
2½ cups flour
½ teaspoon grated lemon peel
¾ teaspoon crushed cardamom

½ cup ground or finely slivered almonds
1 cup currants or raisins
2 tablespoons butter for greasing cookie sheets

1. Preheat oven to 350°.
2. Cream the butter. Blend in the sugar, beating with a wooden spoon until frothy.
3. Whip in the beaten egg.
4. Stir the lemon peel, cardamom, almonds, and currants into the flour.
5. Beat the dry mixture into the sweetened butter.
6. Chill the dough for at least one hour.

7. With well-floured fingers, shape the dough into small balls, about 1″ in diameter, and place them 1″ apart on the greased cookie sheets.
8. Bake between 7 and 10 minutes until golden. Cool on racks, and serve.

MEAT, FISH, AND FOWL

Fruyte Buf—Fruit Beef

2 pounds chuck or other stewing beef cut into ½″ cubes
2 cups ale
2 tablespoons butter
1 tablespoon vegetable or corn oil
1 teaspoon salt
1 pound dates, pits removed
1 cup raisins or dried currants
¾ cup dried apricots, cut into small pieces

1. Place the beef in a mixing bowl and add the ale. Refrigerate overnight.
2. Preheat the oven to 325°.
3. Drain the beef with a colander, but reserve the liquid.
4. Pat the meat dry with paper towels.
5. Heat the butter and oil in a heavy casserole or dutch oven. Brown the meat well on all sides. Sprinkle with salt, and add the dates, raisins, and apricots.
6. Cover the casserole and bake 1½ hours. Occasionally check the meat; to keep it moist, add some of the reserved ale.
7. Spoon the meat onto individual servings of *peppermint rice* (see page 124), and serve piping hot.

Sweet Capon

1 4 to 6 pound capon or roasting chicken
1 pound dates, pits removed
4 tablespoons medium-hot mustard
2 tablespoons rich chicken broth
1 teaspoon dried basil leaves
½ teaspoon salt or less, to taste

1. Preheat the oven to 325°.
2. Set aside 1 tablespoon of mustard.
3. Combine dates, 3 tablespoons mustard, chicken broth, basil, and salt.
4. Stuff the capon with this mixture. Brush the outside of the capon with the reserved mustard.
5. Bake the capon in a covered roasting pan for 1¼–1½ hours or until tender. Remove the cover for the last 10 minutes to permit the skin to become crisp.

Dukess Wynges

24 chicken wings	1 tablespoon honey
1¼ cups whole wheat or all-purpose flour	2 eggs, beaten
½ teaspoon salt	⅛ cup butter, melted
1 tablespoon sugar	⅔ cup milk
1 teaspoon dried basil	¼ cup butter or oil for
1⅛ teaspoons baking powder	sautéing in a frying pan or heavy skillet

1. In a large bowl, mix flour, salt, sugar, basil, and baking powder. In another bowl, mix the honey, egg, butter, and milk.
2. Pour the liquid into the flour mixture, and mix to make a smooth pancake batter.
3. Slowly heat the butter or oil in a frying pan or skillet.
4. Dip each chicken wing in the batter to generously coat it, and slowly sauté the wings in the skillet, about 6 minutes on each side.
5. Remove the browned wings and serve warm.
6. Any leftover batter can be made into small pancakes. Drop the batter 1 teaspoonful at a time into a well-buttered frying pan. When the topside bubbles and the underside is brown, flip each over to briefly brown the other side. Serve with the Dukess Wynges.

Swete Fysshe en Doucette

This easily prepared cold fish and fruit mixture is served in a pastry shell.

Swete Fysshe en Doucette (continued)

24 dried dates, pits removed

2 cups cooked and cooled salmon (or tuna, trout, flounder, haddock, or bass)

⅛ teaspoon salt

⅛ teaspoon freshly ground black pepper, or less to taste

½ cup almonds, finely slivered

½ teaspoon crushed, dried parsley

½ teaspoon crushed, dried rosemary

1 teaspoon ground pine nuts

12 additional dried dates for decoration, pits removed, cut and quartered

12 small sprigs of fresh dill or parsley

12 small baked pastry shells

1. Holding each whole date horizontally on a cutting board, use a small sharp knife to cut date "doughnuts." Moisten the knife frequently to prevent the dates from sticking to it or to one another.
2. In a large mixing bowl, gently stir into the fish the almonds, dates, parsley, rosemary, and pine nuts, plus the salt and pepper.
3. Spoon an equal amount of fish salad into each of the 12 baked pastry shells. These may be filled when cold, or, if you prefer, heated to recrisp them just before filling.
4. Decoratively garnish each with the quartered dates and a sprig of dill or parsley.

RICE AND PASTA

Peppermint Rice

2 cups raw rice

4 cups water

¼ teaspoon salt, more or less to taste

2 tablespoons butter

2 tablespoons firmly packed crushed peppermint leaves, or

2 teaspoons dried peppermint crushed in a mortar with 2 tablespoons crushed fresh parsley

natural green food "paint"

1. In a large, heavy saucepan, combine the rice, water, salt, butter, food coloring, if desired, and peppermint paste. Bring to a quick boil over a high heat.
2. Cover, and simmer until all the liquid is absorbed, about 12 to 15 minutes. The rice should be a delicate green color.

Pasta and Apricot Butter

1 cup dried apricots, cut into tiny pieces	½ pound pasta: spaghetti, broken into small pieces; or macaroni elbows; or noodles
½ cup orange juice	
8 tablespoons butter	
2 tablespoons honey	3 to 4 quarts water
¾ teaspoon cinnamon	1 tablespoon salt
1 teaspoon ground pine nuts	½ tablespoon vegetable oil

1. In an enameled saucepan, heat together the apricots, orange juice, honey, butter, cinnamon, and pine nuts, and simmer very slowly for about 5 minutes.
2. In a large pot, bring the water to a vigorous boil with the salt and oil.
3. Add the pasta, and do not cover. Boil vigorously for 9 to 10 minutes.
4. Drain the pasta thoroughly in a colander and place in a large serving bowl.
5. Pour the apricot butter over the pasta, toss with two forks, and serve hot, immediately.

DELECTABLES

Swithin Cream

A golden lemon and dandelion cream, Swithin Cream is eaten with apple wedges, served upon *chardwardon* (see page 128), or simply as a garnish for dark bread.

Swithin Cream (continued)

2 large lemons
10 yellow dandelion flowers
  or golden squash blossoms
2 cups heavy whipping
  cream

⅛ teaspoon salt
¾ cup sugar

1. Finely grind the rind of the lemons and set aside.
2. Remove the dandelion petals and cut finely with a sharp knife, or carefully cut the squash blossoms into tiny pieces.
3. Gently mix the flowers with the lemon rind.
4. In a medium size mixing bowl, vigorously whip the cream, with a rotary beater, adding the salt and sugar until the cream is thick enough for peaks to stand away from the cream surface.
5. Sprinkle the lemon and dandelion over the cream and carefully mix.

Jusselle Date

1 pound dates, with pits
  removed
4 slices dry date-nut bread
  or gritty brown bread
3 hard-boiled eggs
⅛ teaspoon salt
½ cup ricotta cheese or
  cream cheese

½ cup beef bouillon
2 tablespoons dried sweet
  basil flakes, finely
  crushed
pastry tube with serrated
  nozzle

1. With a sharp, moistened knife, cut each date lengthwise to make a canoe shape suitable for filling. (Place the dates on a damp towel to avoid creating a sticky nuisance.)
2. Chop or pound the bread until it is finely crumbed.
3. With a fork, mash the eggs with the salt and basil.
4. Mix the cheese with half of the bouillon.
5. Blend the egg and cheese mixtures and crumbed bread together.
6. If the mixture is too stiff to easily pass through the pastry tube, add more bouillon.
7. Place the mixture in the pastry tube, and with a gentle but firm hand, decoratively stuff each date.

Almoundyn Eyroun

7 eggs
½ teaspoon salt
¼ cup cream or milk
¼ teaspoon powdered
  saffron
1 tablespoon honey
¾ cup currants or raisins

¾ cup almonds, chopped or
  finely slivered
3 tablespoons butter for
  sautéing in a large frying
  pan or skillet
1 teaspoon dried dill leaves

1. Break the eggs into a mixing bowl and with a fork or rotary beater, vigorously beat them with salt, cream or milk, saffron and honey.
2. Add the currants and chopped almonds to the egg, and vigorously beat again.
3. When the butter in the skillet sizzles, pour the egg mixture into it, and fry for a few minutes until the omelet is set. With a spatula, either fold the circle into a semicircle and brown it lightly on both sides, or flip over the round omelet to brown its opposite side.
4. Cut into wedges, and sprinkle each with dill before serving hot.

FRUITS AND VEGETABLES

Fruyte Fritours

4 large firm pears
4 large apples
2 cups flour
2 eggs
¼ teaspoon salt

2 tablespoons ale, or more
  as needed
¼ pound butter
1½ tablespoons oil
4 tablespoons brown sugar

1. Pare the pears and apples. Cut into quarters and remove the cores and seeds. Then cut into sixteenths, making moon-shaped slices that are firm, not flimsy.
2. Beat the eggs with the salt.
3. Add the eggs and ale to the flour and stir until evenly blended. If the mixture is too dry, add more ale; it should be the consistency of thick pancake batter.

4. Generously coat each apple and pear slice with batter.
5. Heat the butter and oil combination in the skillet. Sauté each crescent until golden brown.
6. With a spatula, remove them to a rack.
7. Sprinkle each fritour with brown sugar while still warm, and serve.

Canel Cucumber

2 large cucumbers   1 teaspoon cinnamon
2 teaspoons sugar

1. Cut the washed cucumbers into ¼″ circles.
2. Thoroughly mix cinnamon with sugar and place the mixture in a salt shaker.
3. Shake cinnamon sugar onto each cucumber round. Decoratively arrange these on a platter and serve.

Chardwardon

A delicious, spicy pear sauce, it is excellent with hard cheese and dark bread, either served alone or garnished with Swithin Cream.

1 lemon, room temperature   ¼ teaspoon nutmeg
8 firm ripe pears   ¾ teaspoon ginger
¾ cup sugar   1 cup water
¼ teaspoon cinnamon   ⅛ teaspoon salt

1. Squeeze the juice from the lemon into a shallow bowl.
2. Cut the pears into quarters, and remove the skin and the cores.
3. Place the pears in the lemon juice to completely cover all surfaces, and set aside.
4. Boil the water with the salt.
5. Drain the pears in a colander, and discard the lemon juice.
6. Add the pears to the boiling water. Stir in the sugar, cinnamon, nutmeg, and ginger. Simmer over a low flame until the pears are soft, about 12 to 15 minutes, stirring several times.
8. Serve warm or cool.

May Sallat

A celebration of fresh greens, this salad unites two main leafy vegetables with green herbs, fruits, and beans.

½ head lettuce, washed and shredded
½ pound spinach, washed and shredded
1 small bunch endive, cut into small pieces
4 stalks fennel, cut into small pieces
1 small bunch parsley, cut into small pieces
7 greengage plums, pits removed, and cut into slivers
1 cup green seedless grapes, each cut into quarters
1 cup fresh peas

½ head broccoli, washed and cut into small flowerettes
1 large lime

SALAD SAUCE:

⅔ cup ricotta cheese
2 tablespoons lime juice
1 cup sour cream or yogurt
1 teaspoon dried sweet basil
2 tablespoons mustard, as spicy as you enjoy it
5 drops green food coloring (made with spinach, the medieval way—see page 116)

1. Place the shredded lettuce and spinach, and the cut endive, fennel, parsley, plums, and grapes in a large decorative bowl.
2. Place the peas and broccoli flowerettes in a small pot with just enough water to cover them and boil for 3 minutes.
3. Drain the vegetables in a colander, discard the water, and when they are slightly cooled, add them to the salad.
4. Grate the lime rind finely, and add it to the salad.
5. With two large spoons or your hands, toss the salad to mix all the greens thoroughly.
6. In a mixing bowl, prepare the salad sauce. Mix the lime juice into the ricotta.
7. In a second bowl, thoroughly mix the mustard and basil into the sour cream or yogurt.
8. Combine the ricotta cheese and cream or yogurt mixtures. If the color is a pleasant, delicate green, fine. If it is not a strong enough hue, add food coloring to make an attractive green sauce.
9. Before serving, pour the sauce over the salad, and lightly toss it.

DRINKS

Mulled Apple or Pear Cider

3 quarts fresh apple cider
  or pear juice
¼ teaspoon nutmeg
⅛ teaspoon thyme

½ teaspoon ginger powder
7 sticks cinnamon
1 tablespoon finely crushed
  dried sweet basil

1. In a large enameled pot, gently simmer the juice with nutmeg, thyme, ginger, and cinnamon sticks.
2. Remove the cinnamon sticks. Break them, placing a portion of stick in each tankard, glass, or chalice. Pour on the warmed cider.
3. Sprinkle sweet basil sparingly on top of each portion.

Lamb's Wool

This gently spiced cider can be made in a variety of ways, so long as the drink has "lamb's wooly" apples and cream floating on its surface. Some medieval recipes suggest baking apples till they burst; others recommend roasting, broiling, or boiling. The apple cider suggested here is not alcoholic; however, some recipes substitute for the cider a dry white wine, a light ale, or stout beer. Depending upon the season for its serving, *lamb's wool* may be drunk warm or cool.

1 gallon apple cider
½ cup sugar, to be added
  if apple cider is very tart
⅛ teaspoon ground nutmeg
¼ teaspoon powdered
  cinnamon
½ teaspoon powdered
  ginger

12 small apples, peeled with
  cores removed
2 cups heavy whipping
  cream
¼ teaspoon salt
2 tablespoons brown sugar

1. In a large enameled pot, slowly heat ¾ of the cider, until warm but not boiling.
2. In another enameled pot pour remaining cider, and add the apples, sugar, nutmeg, cinnamon, and ginger, and bring to a boil. Vigorously simmer the apples until they lose their shape and become "frothy."
3. Pour ¾ of the cider into a large glass serving bowl, which has been slightly heated so that the warm fluid will not crack it.
4. Pour the remaining hot cider with the spiced apples into the serving bowl.
5. Whip the cream with the salt and brown sugar until it peaks.
6. Spoon the cream onto the lamb's wool, or add the cream to each tankard of lamb's wool as it is served.

One cook tastes from a ladle while a heavy pot is raised on a chain and small birds roast on a mechanical spit; the other cook prepares vegetables.

For Further Reading

Some titles (especially the invaluable Wright books) suggest the astonishing vitality of medieval calendar customs in early-modern country life where the calendar has been more important than the clock.

Adams, Joseph Q. *Chief Pre-Shakespearean Dramas.* Boston: Houghton Mifflin, 1924.

Cosman, Madeleine Pelner. *Fabulous Feasts: Medieval Cookery and Ceremony.* New York: George Braziller, 1976, 1978.

————. *Machaut's World: Science and Art in the 14th Century.* New York: New York Academy of Sciences, 1978.

Furnivall, Frederick. *Early English Meals and Manners.* London, 1868; re-issued, Detroit: Singing Tree Press, 1969.

Gairdner, James, ed. *The Paston Letters, 1422–1509.* London: Chatto and Windus, 1904.

Gomme, Alice B. *A Dictionary of British Folklore: Traditional Games.* London: David Nutt, 1894.

Rodgers, Edith C. *Discussion of Holidays in the Later Middle Ages.* New York: Columbia University Press, 1940.

Spicer, Dorothy G. *Yearbook of English Festivals.* New York: W.W. Wilson, 1954.

Strong, Roy. *Splendour at Court.* Boston: Houghton Mifflin, 1979.

Strutt, Joseph. *Sports and Pastimes of the People of England.* London: T. Bensley, 1810; reissued, Detroit: Singing Tree Press, 1968.

Swain, Barbara. *Fools and Folly During the Middle Ages and Renaissance.* New York: Columbia University Press, 1932.

Withington, Robert. *English Pageantry: An Historical Outline.* Cambridge, Mass., 1918; reissued, New York: B. Blom, 1963.

Wright, Arthur, and T.E. Lones, eds. *British Calendar Customs: England.* 3 vols. London: The Folk-Lore Society, William Glaisher, 1936, 1938, 1940.

Sources of Illustrations

p. viii. From Ulrich von Richenthal's *Constanzer Conziliums,* German, 1450–70. New York Public Library, Spencer Ms. 32, p. 87.

pp. 6–7. From the *Luttrell Psalter,* English, c. 1340. British Museum Add. Ms. 42130, f. 207v, f. 208.

p. 10. From Hans Burgkmair, *Der Weisskunig,* German, 15th century. Metropolitan Museum of Art, Gift of Anne and Carl Stein, 1961.

p. 18. From Hans Burgkmair, *Der Weisskunig Jahrbuch,* German, 15th century. Metropolitan Museum of Art, Harris Brisbane Dick Fund, p. 82.

p. 26. From a title page by printer Peter Treveris, London, 1527. Dover Publications, *Alphabets and Ornaments,* p. 39.

p. 28. From J. Hildesheimensis, *Buch der Heilegen drei Konige,* printed by Johann Pruss, Strasbourg, 1500.

p. 29. From P. Drach, *Spiegel der Menschen Behaltniss,* German, 15th century. Metropolitan Museum of Art, Harris Brisbane Dick Fund, 1931.

p. 33. German, 15th century. Metropolitan Museum of Art, Harris Brisbane Dick Fund, 1934.

p. 34. The Emperor of Cathay at Table, German, 15th century. Metropolitan Museum of Art, Bequest of James Clark McGuire, 1931.

p. 38. Print, German, 17th century. Metropolitan Museum of Art, Gift of William Loring Andrews, 1888.

pp. 44–45. From Ulrich von Richenthal, *Constanzer Conziliums,* German, 1450–70. New York Public Library, Spencer Ms. 32, pp. 426–27.

p. 49. From Hans Burgkmair, *Der Weisskunig,* German, 15th century. Metropolitan Museum of Art, Harris Brisbane Dick Fund.

p. 53. From Petrus Crescentius, 15th century. Pierpont Morgan Library M 232, f. 157.

p. 61. From Petrus Crescentius, 15th century. Pierpont Morgan Library M 232, f. 265.

p. 64. Map of Ralph Agas, English, 1560–70, published by London Topographical Society. New York Public Library, Map Room.

p. 68. From C. Grafton, *Historic Alphabets and Initials,* Dover Publications, 1977, p. 66.

p. 71. From Ulrich von Richenthal, *Constanzer Conziliums,* German, 1450–70. New York Public Library, Spencer Ms. 32, p. 71.

p. 74. From Ulrich von Richenthal, *Constanzer Conziliums,* German, 1450–70. New York Public Library, Spencer Ms. 32, p. 56.

p. 79. From the *Da Costa Hours,* Bruges, 1520. Pierpont Morgan Library M 399, f. 11v.

p. 82. From Ulrich von Richenthal, *Constanzer Conziliums,* German, 1450–70. New York Public Library, Spencer Ms. 32, pp. 114–15.

p. 85. From the *Da Costa Hours,* Bruges, 1520. Pierpont Morgan Library M 399, f. 8v.

pp. 88–89. From Gregory's *Moralia,* 12th century. Paris, Bibliothèque Nationale, Ms. Latin 15675, f. 8v.

p. 91. Hans Weiditz, for Cicero's *Officia,* Ausburg, 1531. Metropolitan Museum of Art, Gift of Felix M. Warburg, 1918.

p. 93. From M. Wohlgemuth, *Der Schatzbehalter,* Nuremburg, 1491. Galeria Medievalia, London.

p. 97. From the *Da Costa Hours,* Bruges, 1520. Pierpont Morgan Library M 399, f. 13v.

p. 102. From *Spiegel der menschlicher Behaltnis,* published by Peter Drach, Speyer, 1500.

p. 111. From Hans Burgkmair, *Der Weisskunig,* German, 15th century. Metropolitan Museum of Art, Harris Brisbane Dick Fund, 1943.

p. 131. From Froschauer in Diederich's *Deutsches Leben I,* #574, German, 16th century. Metropolitan Museum of Art, Rogers Fund.

Index

The detailed table of contents on pages v–vii will also be useful for locating specific references.